UNREMARKABLE

A.J. SCHMITZ

MAXIXAM
PRESS

Dedicated to the doctors and nurses
I met on the road to recovery.

Other books by A.J. Schmitz:

Buggin' Out

The Death of Our Dreams: And Other Funny Stories

Nut Job

The Stupid Machine

Ruuning the Four-Minute Mile: And Other Delusions

Dear Norman: A collection of stupid, funny and absurd emails sent to companies... and the replies.

Stocking Stuffers: Holiday Memoirs & Musings

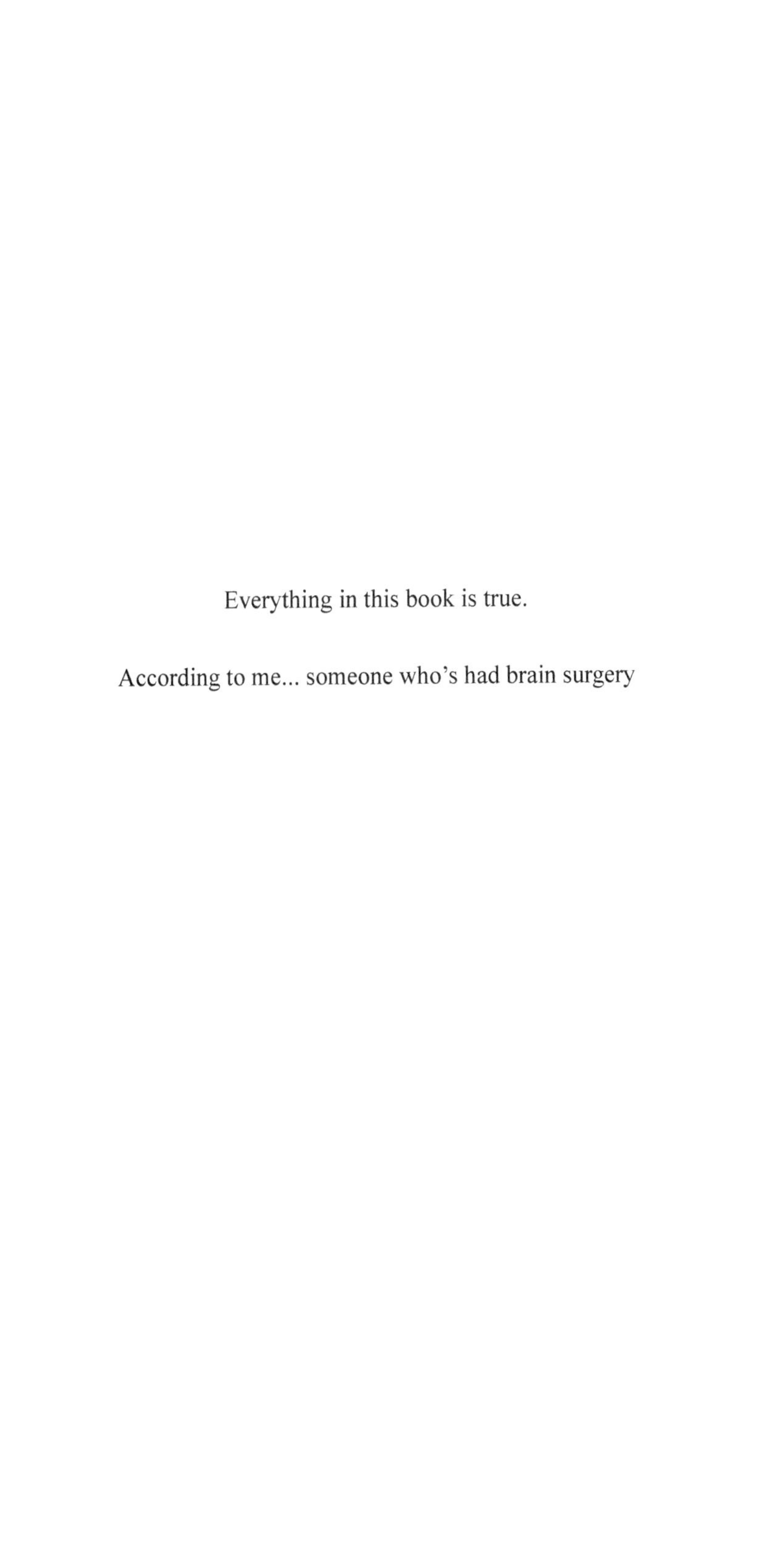

Everything in this book is true.

According to me... someone who's had brain surgery

CONTENTS

Fair Retail

SATURDAY

10:30 am

I'm sitting at the book fair, hocking my wares in the rain. It hasn't rained in months, but the second I show up at the book fair – rain! I'm praying for the *rain rain to go away and come back another day*, but according to everyone I meet, "we really need the rain." I get it. Water is important. We need it to survive. The dirt around here is drying into worthless clay. It's bad. May showers will likely bring June flowers, but I won't care because I'll be at the beach baking like bacon and not giving a shit about one mother-fragrant flower.

When I joined the book fair five weeks ago, it seemed like a brilliant idea. "I'll sell a million books" I thought – like most delusional writers think. All the hustling I do on-line doesn't work because there's 10 billion people hustling their shit online, making the internet a virtual marketplace of screaming monkeys habitually posting the same thing over and over and over again. Like a broken record; although no one knows what a record is anymore, so we should compare it to broken backend computer code that an AI machine repeats until it's a smoking heap of springs and deadly metals poisoning the environment.

Now that I'm here at the campus of Long Island University, I don't necessarily regret my decision, but book buyers don't like getting caught in the rain – regardless of what that *Pina Colada Song* says. Books get damaged in water. They buckle and warp and the pages stick together. Spending good money on things that can't be used is pointless, even though we constantly buy useless garbage. It's the basis of our economy!

I have a sign taped to a pole on my 10x10 tent that educates people about my books and authors similar to me. This is so people don't need to speak to me if they don't want to – and most of them don't want to. The sign does the work. They can read the sign, which is what people at this event enjoy doing… reading. I have all my books on stands and flowered across the table like a colorful bouquet of June flowers. The covers are snazzy, eye-catching, and fun. I designed them myself. No one seems to give a shit. The only guy interested in my books so far was a writer who thought I was a publisher and told me about the Cold War book he wrote, which he claimed no one was interested in, and he was right because the second I heard the subject matter my brain snapped off like an old transistor radio.

I got back from Boston the night before and I'm a little groggy. I drank too much wine, and I made the mistake of traveling with my parents there and back. They were in good spirits, but my father lost his marbles the second we got off the Throggs Neck Bridge to Long Island. Traffic was knotted like a crocheted sweater, and it took us an additional two hours to get home, a trip that normally takes about 40 minutes.

Again, I'm not regretful to enter the fair as a vendor, but I have a feeling my time and money are being wasted. People aren't strolling as much as rushing through like they're headed to a better destination than my table. The girls selling cookies across the brick walkway are doing okay though, because cookies are in constant demand. Cookies are recession-proof, diet-proof, and apparently rain-proof.

11:30 am

The rain has come and gone in waves. The skies are finally clear and it's surprisingly cool. It was humid and funky an hour ago, but now it's breezy and bright – the sky blanketed in a veil of white clouds.

I don't normally judge people by their appearance. Look at the occasional buttoned-up politician who votes for conservative policies, then gets caught in an airport restroom with their pants around their ankles, getting a blowjob from a homeless person desperate for a few bucks. But you can definitely judge the people at this fair. Most of them shuffling through look as though they haven't left their homes in months other than to get food and peruse book fairs. These people are incapable of making eye contact, conversing in octaves above a peep, or functioning normally in any conceivable way. They're generally considered shut ins.

Introverts.

Terrified introverts.

They're interested in candles, hippie clothing, 15-dollar jewelry, and the booth selling color prints of famous images like Rosie the Riveter and that French woman in front of a circular art nouveau hanging garden thing. There's a woman walking around dressed as a butterfly. I assume someone hired her to be here. There's a bouncy castle, and a children's story tent where people are spinning in circles like Hare Krishnas. I think I made a terrible mistake.

I suppose I can chalk this experience up as precious *me* time – time to sit for six hours and get some peaceful writing done, with no one to bother me – especially shoppers. Which is exactly what's happening. My family is not around, there's no chores to do, and the fresh air will do me good – I suppose. I can sit and reflect on the choices I've made in my life thus far. My decision to write books, my decision to market them myself… the choice to come to this dead zone on a Saturday when I could be doing a million other things – like watching TV, or mowing the lawn which grew 10 inches since I went to Boston.

11:55 am

Someone *actually* picked up my book, fanned it open, and feigned interest. I gave a brief summary of who I was and what I write, but that info went in one ear and out the other. The only other action I've gotten is a dog pissing on a lamp post roughly eight feet away. Besides that, no one cares. I've spoken to two people. I can't get anyone to even stop and look at a book. Barely a glance. I've worn my least intimidating beach shirt, and my hair is as soft and windblown as a school-teacher. Thank God I brought a giant thermos of coffee, or I'd be borderline suicidal over this.

When I first arrived, a security guard forced me to park a mile away, so I hauled my shit to the other side of the giant lawn to my spot. My shoes got wet in the morning dew. A book fair employee named Alice lent me her wagon while she hauled my 6-foot table over herself. "I just don't want to throw out my back again," she proclaimed, dragging the thing like Igor the hunch-back assistant. I told her I could do it, but she insisted. I believe I heard her vertebrae snap like packing bubbles. I've since seen her running back and forth a few times, each time appearing more confused and bent over than the last.

12:30 pm

A man of great intelligence *finally* purchased my book *Buggin' Out*. He initially came around and snooped, then asked about my books while I spit my spiel like a used car salesman. That's what you need to do at these things, prac-tically jump across the table and strangle these people. Then he left. I figured he was one of the many fish that would wig-gle off the hook, but he returned. He's giving *Buggin' Out* to his friend Jerry as a birthday gift. He wanted me to sign it, so I did. Conjuring deep into my soul for something witty to say, I managed to scribble, "Jerry, Happy Birthday!" with my unique signature under it. I'm sure once Jerry sees those hilarious words of wisdom, he'll dive right in.

2:35 pm

After a small wave of interest, the tides have turned back to nothing. I printed bookmarks with pictures of my books displayed quaintly on a wooden shelf on one side, and all pertinent information on the flip side, including a QR code. It's about the only thing people have taken, and half of them have done so reluctantly. They stuff it in their sweaty palms and crush it like a CVS receipt. It's bleak. Not only am I down a side "street" from the main walkway, but I'm also realizing this is barely a book fair. Yes, staff are wearing matching shirts with the book fair's name emblazoned across them, but book sellers make up perhaps 20% of the stands. The rest is lemonade, trinkets, and booths asking to support a cause. People actually *drove* to this place to be here.

3:00 pm

The butterfly girl is now on stilts. She's at least 12 feet in the air. I wish I was that high too. The tides turn again and suddenly there's people around, sniffing around like old dogs. I sell a few books. I've decided I'm not going to commit the cardinal sin of book buying and cast it upon the roaming shoppers, and that is: "judging a book by its cover." After having a marathon yap session with the woman in the booth next to me selling her book about school bullying, two nondescript women come right over to me, and one of them purchased two books from me. *Nut Job* and *Dear Norman*. It's official. I have no idea what people want, who my customers are, or what they find appealing about my writing. I recently received a four-star rating on Goodreads from an elderly Midwest woman with 1960s bee-hive hair. I give up.

3:30 pm

The sun is falling through the trees. It's sunny and warm. The coffee has worn off and now I'm guzzling water. I ask the woman next to me if she could watch my booth so I could use the bathroom. She said, "of course." She's nice. We've exchanged bits of conversation throughout the day. Her tent is bright yellow, with magenta walls to match her book cover. Her hair is magenta too. It's like someone spilled a bucket of paint chip samples for a unicorn-themed bedroom. I borrowed my buddy Stephen's tent, which is blue and saggy. I went with brown tablecloth covers because I wanted the appearance of wood and a sort of "library" feeling. Having returned from using the bathroom, I see from a distance my choice of brown, which is closer to vomit orange, and the green signs I made bearing my name, gives shoppers the impression I may be color blind. When I tell book browsers that I design my own book covers, they are impressed, but it's the kind of impressed that only makes them nod their head, an action slightly more animated than the rigor mortis they displayed seconds before.

4:00 pm

The shoppers came and went with the schedule of the

guest speakers holding court inside the buildings. There were some slightly famous writers speaking at various places and at various times, but I never bothered to find out who they were, nor did I bother to get a schedule booklet because all I care about is myself. I couldn't give a shit about who sold what, as long as I got some action. I don't say things like that *out loud* because it's not polite. I even encouraged magenta woman when she sold her first book of the day, a $45 tomb that's difficult to push, but I genuinely wish all shoppers would come to me and ignore everyone else. It's shitty karma, but if you only THINK this stuff, it doesn't come back to haunt you.

4:15 pm

As the day comes to a close, a young woman, or perhaps, an older teen comes to my booth. She's snarkier than me, if that's possible. Her girl friend, or perhaps, her girlfriend, asks for six bucks so she can get something to eat. Snarky girl stuffs some bills in her hand and feigns anger after she leaves. "All she wants is my money," she huffs in a mock tone. I describe my books in detail, and her smirk lets me know it's right up her alley. After much debate, she buys two books. *Dear Norman* and *The Stupid Machine.* She loves the cover for *Stupid,* and when I tell her I designed all the book covers myself, she says, "you need a raise." I love this girl. She's essentially me 35 years ago except with a vagina. From the looks of it, we may have the same taste in women. She pays with Venmo. I have a sheet with QR codes for all money exchange systems. Venmo, Zelle, PayPal and more links to my books on Amazon, but Venmo is the only QR used. In fact, it was the payment method choice of the day. I went to the bank right before I came to the fair and got a wad of $1s and $5s, but now that they've gone unused, I'll be paying for everything, regardless of price, in tiny denominations.

She's my second to last sale of the day. I sell one to Magenta who buys a *Buggin' Out*, and I give her a *Dear Norman* for free. She gives it to her husband, who's quietly standing ground behind a mask of wraparound sunglasses and long grey beard. He dives right into *Norman*, turning occasionally to tell me the responses to the funny emails "are precious." It's a fine final send off.

4:45 pm

I slowly break down my stand piecemeal and run it the two football fields to the car in the parking lot. It takes five trips. Rita informed me we were having dinner with friends at 6:00. I leave the books displayed to the last second thinking I'll miss the guy who would no doubt wander by at 4:58 and purchase 30 books, but couldn't because I left at 4:57.

NEXT DAY

SUNDAY

11:00 am

Today's the second day of the book fair. Starting later, 11:00 am, I drive 20 minutes from my house into the small town of Oyster Bay to find the streets quarantined by security cars with flashing yellow lights. Tents are rising in the distance. After a careful examination of their "documents," the people running the "book fair" don't have me listed as a seller, but the main woman remembers me from yesterday and kicks me to the curb at some awkward spot in front of a nondescript brick building… maybe a bank or some soulless paper-pushing business. No one would pretend they paid to come here and sell books. I actually *did* pay to come here and sell books, which is even sadder. Whether the author is paying for a booth spot, or sneaking in and securing a booth spot, selling books here is a futile experience. That's my life in a nutshell.

I'm lucky enough to unload at my spot and park at the train station nearby. My son Max is with me today. He's my right-hand man. He dropped his cell phone last week, which shattered more than it was already shattered from the last time he dropped it, so now he can't mindlessly scroll through the book-killing internet, and is spending time with his old man. Who thought giving kids $1,000 handheld minicomputers was a good idea? Now his mind is free to talk with me and enjoy the frustrations of selling books at a street fair.

11:30 am

It's not raining! It's sunny and bright – but, windy *as hell*. It's been a half hour into this shitshow, and Max has complained about the wind thirty times. A complaint per minute. After a while I tell him to stop, but he's right, it's obnoxious. The girls selling crappy t-shirts across the street have lost their tent twice – both times a stranger rescuing it from literally killing someone. The fair people emphasized proper tent security in their guidelines, and these girls did not abide but the strict letter of the law. I'd actually enjoy seeing a tent kill someone today. It may liven up the place. Our properly secured tent is next to a woman selling cheap jewelry and the woman next to her is selling artisan cookies. Again, more cookies.

This was listed as the second day of the book fair, but I'd say maybe 10% of the people are selling books today. The rest is junk. I'm not on a side "street" like yesterday, but I'm on the "elbow" of a bend down a side street, so to view my booth you need to go against a natural walking flow and most people are not interested in fighting the current.

12:30 pm

There was nothing to eat for breakfast because the last gluten-free waffles went to Max, and I ate one fried egg, so I'm starving. Max ran to the deli a few doors down to scope out the grub. It's a Spanish takeout restaurant that caters mostly to Central and South American landscapers. Max and I love that food, so I ask Max to get us some tamales. He doesn't want to go, so I go because absolutely nobody is coming to my booth. I get tamales, which are pork, and return to eat them with Max. I was gone *maybe* four minutes, and when I return, Max informs me two groups came to my table. I asked him what he said, and he mumbled to *me* that he mumbled to *them* something about these being "my dad's books." Not exactly a salesman. He's 15. No one his age speaks an octave above boots on gravel. I get mad because I asked him to get food so I could watch the booth, and now he sees that I'm right. Doesn't matter.

1:00 pm

Our tamales are disappointing. They were over seasoned, and the meat inside was 90% crushed bones. I know these landscapers work hard and are starving for lunch, but they can't possibly be eating bones for lunch. Max contemplates the many snack stands that litter the place. Since this book fair is really a street fair, the choices are plenty.

Max and I talk about basketball as the Knicks have advanced to the Eastern Conference Finals, and Max wore his Knicks sweatshirt. Occasionally, someone either shouts *Knicks!* or comes up to tell us their philosophy to winning this series against the Indiana Pacers. Everyone's an expert, apparently, including us – regurgitating every dumb rant we've heard on ESPN, or any number of sports talk shows before, during, and after the games. One old man walks up with a vintage 1994 Finals cap when the Knicks played the Houston Rockets for the Chip, so Max and I return the favor we'd received many times over the day and yell "Knicks" to the man. He stares at us terrified and stumbles away. I believe he may be a missing person.

2:00 pm

After a few stragglers come by and I sell a few books, there's a long dry spell. Like yesterday, the people come in waves. It's after lunch and there's numerous people about, yet none are buying books. Max and I have analyzed every person walking by at this point, and we understand completely who's shopping for books and who's not buying books at all. It's a sociological study of human behavior and patterns.

Let's start with who's NOT buying books from me:
- Anyone essentially using the street as a sidewalk and zipping through fast
- Young couples in gym clothes
- Couples of any age holding massive, sweating plastic Dunkin' iced coffee cups
- Couples holding only their cell phones
- Anyone walking a dog
- Anyone with a child
- Old people who look lost, confused, or guiding each other in the opposite direction the other was intending to go
- Any male between the age of 0 and 18
- Anyone eating something that requires a spoon
- Large groups of people stumbling around a fair because that's what people do at fairs
- Any female who stopped to yap with the two female romance novelists across from me
- Anyone wearing more than one article of New York Yankees, Mets, Knicks, Rangers, or Islanders clothing

- People dressed as security, whether it's for this event or not.
- Anyone squinting *really* hard
- People frowning so as not to be peddled to
- Anyone holding a bag from the aforementioned jewelry shops and artisan cookies stands.

People who ARE buying books from me, or at the very least, browsing:

- Anyone holding an eco-friendly canvas bag over their shoulder
- People who *actually* come to my table
- People who are smiling
- Any woman over 50 who is frantic, world-weary, yet has an excellent sense of humor.
- Men similar to the women above, but are acting like they're not buying, but kinda buying.
- Gen Xers, Millennials and Gen Zers who are dressed fashionably

2:30 pm

There's an hour and a half left to this fair and it feels hopeless. Max's dream of exceeding the 7 books I sold the day before will be dashed. We'll be lucky to sell one more than the 4 we've barely sold today. To make up for the pain, Max ran off the get donuts from the donut food truck.

The donut truck feels like the antithesis of the book fair's intended philosophy. Besides the fair being marketed and sold as a book fair, there's hardly any book sellers, although I found out later during a stroll that the main sponsor is a bookstore in town that has a *massive* book table outside their bookshop selling piles of books, which stymies small book sellers like me. But the "book" fair is, in reality, just a street fair selling stuff you'd see at ANY street fair, but all the small artisan sweet stands are being overshadowed by the donut truck, which is selling fresh hot donuts made to order with steaming cups of coffee. There's an endless line to wait for them. Who can compete with that? It's a kick in the balls for those of us who rely on a fair like this to get the word out. The people walking around this fair seem only interested in getting out of the house and nothing more. They didn't come for books. They came out because they've been sitting in their fucking living rooms for five months and are going stir crazy.

Max returns to give me a cup of coffee from the donut truck, which is outstanding, so now I secretly love the donut truck, and I'm a horrible turncoat against my fellow artisan sellers and independent writing brethren. Sorry.

3:00 pm

A young couple walk up who meet almost every criteria Max and I have created for potential book buying. They're a Millennial couple, smiling, dressed sharply and holding canvas bags. She comes first and after I pitch her, she suggests he may like what I'm selling. After a brief overview, he buys a *Dear Norman* and a *Nut Job*. I give them a bookmark. Max is thrilled. I'm happy too.

4:00 pm

The day is over, but it really ended an hour before.

I run to get the car. I ask a security guard if I can bring my car in and load my stuff. He's not sure. No one has told him anything over the radio, and he can't answer any of my questions about loading, driving, or entrance into the restricted area. He's the opposite of the security guy from yesterday who was demanding and full of false bravado. I tell him I'll go up a side street, and sneak down through the barriers into my spot. He agrees that's a good idea. Apparently public safety is only a concern if someone is telling you things over a hand radio.

The day ends mercifully. We sell 6 books today. 13 in total for the weekend. It's a miserable haul for the two days of work I put in. The only saving Grace is Max and I spending Sunday together and having a wonderful time. We've analyzed humans and their strange behaviors, both good and bad, which is always fun, but we also talked about his great love basketball, and peppered in bits of life philosophy. Although not surprising, Max is incredibly observant and reflective about life. It was enough to help me endure a rather disappointing sales stream.

Hey… there's always next year.

Writing Tips!

You want to become a writer? You've come to the right place.

Some consider *Stephen King on Writing* to be the shining source of writing advice. Bullshit. It's better served as a firestarter than a book of quality writing tips. Tear it into confetti and continue reading below.

The art of writing isn't so much about the inspiration, but the discipline to do it. For that I recommend heavy doses of cocaine and if available, methamphetamines. I'm kidding. Coffee and tequila will do just fine. Fill a mug of each and get in front of the computer.

Note: Stephen King wrote something in the neighborhood of 15 books in two years on cocaine, all of them bestsellers. Take that into consideration.

Find a quiet place to write. Jail is the perfect setting. If you're not in jail, consider a non-violent crime… maybe fraud or grand larceny. Once locked in a cell, you'll have nothing but free, uninterrupted time to write. If your cellmate is insane, ask a guard if the library is available. If not, consider hitting another inmate over the head with a dumbbell. You'll get tossed into solitary confinement where it's incredibly quiet.

Once you've settled in, get to work. Some people write in longhand on paper. That process needs to stop immediately. Get a computer. If you can't type, learn to type. If you don't have a computer, date someone who does. Even if you need to get into a homosexual (or heterosexual) relationship. The hotter they are, the better. I'm talking about their hardware. Their facial looks don't matter. Put a bag over their head and do what you need to do to get some time on their computer.

They say you should write for at least 15 minutes a day. I say, do about 15 hours a day. Don't stop until you crash into a sobbing ball. It's okay. These low points create good art. Just make sure you can clear the tears away so you can see the computer monitor. Then, type away until the sun comes up. Try and rest if you can. If you're in bed, stay there. If you're not in bed, drop where you are. Even if you're in line for coffee. Don't worry, people will step over you. They need their coffee and a small bump on the floor is a minor inconvenience to them.

Note: It's often recommended to write every day. That's terrible advice. You need plenty of time to procrastinate so you spiral into a series of panic attacks that fuel inconsistent styles.

Treat your writing like a job. Get up, eat breakfast and fall into miserable despair. If you work from home, drive around the block and get into a traffic jam. Yell at other drivers. It simulates typical work life. Once home, write until you need either food, water or medication. Medication is expensive and probably not covered in your health plan, so I recommend tequila. You'll find it everywhere. No insurance necessary.

I talk a lot about coffee and tequila. Both of those things are plentiful in Mexico. Go there if necessary. Mexicans seem to be leaving in droves; why not go there? Should be pretty empty. Find a place by the beach. Listen to the surf hit the shore. You may be sleeping there if your writing doesn't pay. Sand is soft like a pillow. The nights are fairly warm. A fish may swim up and you can eat it.

Find a muse. Someone or something that gets into your veins and inspires you to write. I recommend teq… sorry, force of habit… I recommend a lover. That special someone who drives you insane. When they're not distracting you with their petty needs, they'll drive you mad with their selfishness. Write about it when they're passed out. Maybe dive into a love triangle. Make your life as complicated as possible. Repeat if necessary.

Note: Make sure you listen to as much criticism as possible from people not important to you in any way. Disregard criticism from loved ones, editors and experts. You know what's best!

A good writer should read a lot. Try the job ads. You

need money. Writing doesn't pay very well, or at all, really. Most writers die poor in the gutter. The ones that don't wish they did. The best industry for writers to work is someplace where they're not seen or heard – like, a security guard in a basement or a tollbooth operator on the night shift. There's plenty of time to contemplate what to write while staring into a dark void.

A good writer should also be filled with self-doubt. If you're prancing around like you own the earth, there's a good chance you're a terrible writer. Practice nervous energy, self-loathing, fear, and the occasional mental breakdown. If you can't pretend to do these things, act like it. If there's one thing a good writer is besides being a good writer… it's being a good actor.

Note: Punctuation is almost completely unnecessary as are poor structure extraneous words that basically literally do nothing to enhance the story and never-ending run-on sentences filled with a ridiculously high amount of adverbs. Stephen King says: "the road to hell is paved with adverbs." Remember, we're ignoring that hack millionaire's advice.

A good writer should have awful habits. Don't bite your nails. It's difficult to type with bloody stumps. Smoking and self-harm are preferable, but try drugs or lying. Before you know it, your life is in shambles. Fortunately, you can mine some great material from the lies and misery you've created. Isn't that what good fiction is all about? The truth?

Once you have a good outline, notes, and character development, light it all on fire. Toss it away. Wing it. Improvised writing is the best. It seems fresher when you make it up as you go. Do little research and make up your own rules. If it's not pointless drivel by the time you're done, you're doing it all wrong. Fix it in the edit.

Note: Walk away from your work and 'let it breath.' Look at it later with fresh eyes. That way, when you read it again, you can ask: "Who wrote this garbage?"

Finally, market your work endlessly – even if it isn't good. Put it up on Facebook, your website, your blog, and on your mother's refrigerator. All the places everyone ignores. You're bound to be successful. If not, try the gutter. It's not the most ideal place to be, but you'll have plenty of company.

Sick as a Dog

I was sick today so I stayed home from work. I don't get sick much. I rarely miss work whether I'm hungover like a sailor or awaken with a nasal cavity impacted with crusted phlegm.

I was blessed with good health and thinness, something I didn't appreciate until I got older. I went to school often because of good health. When at school, I was often told I was skinny.

"You're so skinny," kids would holler at me as they picked up my arm to examine like a scarf dangling across a mannequin. "Do you ever eat?"

No one ever thinks about the consequences of calling someone skinny. Especially a boy. Perhaps they think it's a compliment, or something that needs to be pointed out because we lacked mirrors in our home. No one goes up to another person, caresses their cheek and says, "you're so ugly." And God-forbid we tell someone they're fat.

"Wow! You're so fat!" How do you think that would go over in polite company? "Do you ever stop eating?"

Now that I'm older, I'm *thin*… that's a polite way of saying I'm in decent shape and not a fat-ass like many people my age.

"Well, you're thin…" is a common response I hear in conversations now. That's usually proceeded by another statement like, "…so, you can fit into those jeans" or, "…you can eat that bacon double cheeseburger." Apparently, no one knows about cholesterol.

My thinness has kept the stress off my knees and back. I work out, which helps me stay fit. It also stems sickness. I'm sick so infrequently, I become concerned when I'm sick.

"This is the end now, isn't it?"

It starts with a little sniffle and cuts to a tragic scene of my family crying in fits next to a hospital bed while I waste away.

I hate being sick. Most people do. I hate it because I sit in my house and look at all the shit that needs to get done around my house.

"I could be hanging that picture on the wall, but I feel awful." *Those patio chairs need to be power washed, but I can't do that sick! I'll get more sick!!* Then, once I'm healthy, I'm at work. I can't do choirs at work because I'm working. The cycle never ends.

When I was a kid, sick days meant burrowing into the couch, watching *The Price is Right* and drinking soup. Now when I'm sick, my wife makes me do chores. She gets sick less than I do. She *never* gets sick, so when I get sick, she insists I'm being some kind of pussy and should tackle the chore list that's longer than Santa's naughty list. I get no soup… no *Price is Right*. In fact, if I get sick, I have to get my *own* soup. Sometimes I need to make it myself – from scratch! That's because I make awesome chicken soup. My wife says, "You're sick? You should make your delicious chicken soup!" It's a good idea but my soup takes 3 hours to make, and I'll be dead before I finish making it. She wants to enjoy my soup and she's not even sick.

Many people get sick in a specific place on their body. Some get frequent ear infections or stomach aches. My mother gets laryngitis. I get weird nose colds that cycle from clogged–to empty raw–to clogged again. They alternate, so one side is clogged, and the other side is empty raw, then without warning, they swap. Then, they partner and do a full clog. The ears eventually join in. In the morning I'm deaf, by afternoon my hearing echoes like a rock cavern. I also get sore throats. It's a double edge sword because I'm one of those unusual people who get super hungry when they're sick. Most people's appetites disappear when sick, but I become ravenous. I empty the fridge into my face. I eat things that doctors normally tell you to shy away from.

"Eat light broths and drink tea," they say.

I eat cold cut sandwiches with melting cheese, topped with at *least* three condiments. I wash it down with orange juice, a bowl of corn flakes and something random like chocolate covered coffee beans or spoons of peanut butter sprinkled with paprika. It's the diet of a pregnant person. I suppose the body is asking for vitamins; but why take vitamins when you can enjoy peanut butter with paprika? It's hard to eat the volume of food I consume with a sore throat. Every swallow is like a sword going down. With every thick mouthful that drops, my face resembles someone kicked in the nether region. If I eat light broths, I'll be hungry before I set the spoon down.

People say they're "sick as a dog" which means nothing to me. Dogs seem to get over sickness quickly. Dogs puke, look at it, then contemplate eating it or taking a nap. Maybe napping is what dogs do well. I can't sleep well when I'm sick. I try, but I watch bad movies instead. I usually wait until I'm exhausted, then head off to bed where I stare at the ceiling, wide awake and unable to sleep. I believe I do the opposite of most people when sick. I do chores, eat a ton of heavy food, and stay up all night. It's all backwards. Thank God I'm thin.

I've left a lot of tissues bunnies around the house today. They build up like snowball piles. My wife won't touch them. I don't blame her. Grab one incorrectly and it can pop like an overcooked soup dumpling. Rita has a serious dislike to snot. Especially to other people's. She gags at the thought of it. Her entire family has the gag reflex of a nervous bulimic. Her brother once found a hair in his food and projectile vomited onto the table. At a restaurant. What's worse? A hair in your food or a bucket of vomit across the entire table?

When I'm sick, one minute I'm about to die – the next, I feel fine. Sickness seems to come in waves. I awaken feeling like death warmed over, then 10 minutes after calling in sick to work, I feel totally fine. I think to myself, "I probably *could* have gone to work today." Then after lunch, I crash like a sorority freshman after an all-night keg bender.

•••

I went to work sick today. It was the biggest mistake of my life. Or at least very close to it. I've made some questionable choices, but going to work sick is high on the list. I feel like death warmed-over, yet I also feel obligated to go in. We're crushed at work, and I have a disturbing sense of loyalty to a company that would most likely replace me in seconds. They'd download 50 resumés before I was cold in the ground.

"Hi yes, we're hiring. Our last Creative Director? I'm standing over him right now."

I try and fool my body into thinking I just got off the phone after calling in sick to replicate the feeling I get after doing it at home, but it doesn't work. The home call was made on a foamy couch. I'm on hard office furniture under harsh lighting with no escape to any sort of bedding. The sense of home security is what gives relief. Even if I'm forced to make chicken soup from scratch.

People come and go from my office and ask questions. Why do they ask so many questions? Do they always ask so many questions? Or do they compound in annoyance when sick? I can't answer these questions because I'm sick. People usually linger in my office just as I need to blow my nose. Of course, I need to be cordial and smile — eliminate any idea that I'm infecting everyone within a 10-foot radius. Once alone, I empty my nasal passage into a paper towel like a faucet.

On my second breakfast of the morning, I contemplate the next six hours I need to be trapped here. I may run out of food. In the morning, most people believe they're bringing enough food for lunch but find they've under packed. That's because they pack with a full stomach. I pack with future hunger in mind. I bring a cooler big enough for the beach and pack it to the brim with vittles. Second breakfast, lunch, snack… snack number two. I'm like a Hobbit with a mid-level job.

I work and eat simultaneously. Stuffing an orange wedge in the mouth while using a computer mouse *and* typing is a skill not many people can do. I'm an expert because I haven't taken a lunch break in 25 years. I'm still trying to master keeping food off my shirt while multi-tasking. Maybe in 25 years I'll get the swing of it.

People make fun of my large lunch container, but will no doubt run to me when the apocalyptic mushroom clouds burst outside the office windows, and the sky turns the color of my orange wedges.

"Oh, you're hungry? My massive lunch container isn't so funny now, is it?"

People see my lunch box and judge me. They think, "You're one of those guys!" They mean, *those lucky people who can eat a literal horse and not get fat*. There's nothing worse, at least for me, than food regret.

"Damn, I was going to toss that leg of lamb in my cooler, but I didn't!"

I don't want to get caught in a meeting with a rumbling stomach. Especially when I'm sick. My body is like a drag race car when sick. I need to fill it with gas just to zoom 100 yards. Then it needs a refill for race number two. Most people get a rumbling belly when hungry, but for some reason, my stomach squeaks. Like someone rubbing an inflated balloon with wet hands. Then, there's the inevitable exchange of looks around the conference table.

"Was that you or me?" they ask, because the stomach noises tend to come from unknown origins. Like a ventriloquist. I immediately admit it's me. Then, the squeaks turn to B-movie horror moans. *Wooaaaooo…* a sound bite from a *Scooby Doo* cartoon.

"You okay?" I'm fine. I'm thin!

The afternoon is a wash of grey. Grey mind and earl grey tea. I'm pretty sure I did work, but I can't say what it was – or if it was done correctly. The same people who were in my office today will be in my office asking me questions on Monday and I won't be able to answer them properly. *Monday A.J.* will be a completely different person than *Today A.J.* – *Monday A.J.* will need to answer for all the terrible misguided decisions *Sick A.J.* made, most of them executive decisions based on kicking the proverbial can down the road for *Healthy A.J.* to deal with. *Healthy A.J.* will not appreciate it one bit.

I will say I was sick, but it won't matter. No one cares. Poor work is not a good excuse in the eyes of the healthy. The only things I'll remember in the flashback is lunch, a few snippets of conversation, and how much I desperately needed to be home. I'll need to explain my shoddy work, and justify half-assed decisions.

Hopefully, all will be forgiven when our clients confess that the deadlines they gave us were unrealistic and inflated for no reason whatsoever.

•••

Now I'm sick on the weekend. There's nothing worse than being sick on the weekend. Maybe homelessness, or starvation. It's a short list! People think I'm starving myself because I'm so thin. But I eat. Especially when hungry… and sick. Week*ends* are when we do all the things we can't do during the week*days* because we're enslaved at work.

Being sick during the work week gives one a small sense of joy. No one likes work, and being sick is the only acceptable excuse to miss work because no one wants to be infected with your germs. Call in to your office to tell them your mom died or you're in a car accident, and they'll await your arrival any minute. Say you're sick, and they know you'll infect everyone… unless you work in a different department. Then they'll make you drag your ass in.

When I was a kid, I faked being sick. I was a good actor so I could pull it off. My mother would let me slide occasionally. She knew the benefits of a personal day or two.

One of the benefits of being sick is cold medicine.

Three or four of those little plastic cups of NyQuil and that restless sleep you had the night before is a distant memory. Most likely because your memory is wiped away from its active ingredients. Before you can finish reading the synopsis of that Netflix show you've been meaning to watch, you'll be drooling like a psych ward patient after a few sessions of electro-shock therapy.

When I lived in Manhattan, I went to a doctor around the corner when I had a terrible cough I couldn't shake. I didn't have a regular doctor, so I dug up this guy somehow. The secretary gave me an appointment for noon that day, which was

15 minutes from when I dialed the phone. I sprinted to the appointment and coughed in her face.

The secretary was 70 years-old, but the doctor was 90. He resembled dust modeled into a person. He examined me for 10 seconds, then prescribed a giant bottle of cough syrup with codeine. Best week of my life. The codeine left me in a hallucinatory stupor most people travel to Mexico to achieve. The doctor was old school. Codeine cough syrup, cocaine for toothaches, and the occasional hole drilled in the head to release the demons.

For some reason, opiates stop coughing. So does alcohol. My buddy Voytek, who always functioned at illegal blood alcohol levels, would inevitably recommend a shot of vodka with pepper as a stopgap for illnesses. Especially coughs. I usually wait until I'm well to start drinking again. Hard alcohol at least.

If you're like me, the effects of NyQuil lasts roughly four hours until I awaken in a pool of sweat, wondering where I am. I get up at God knows what hour, stumble to the bathroom in the dark, and take another shot. It's a questionable decision because I'll be a zombie in the morning, but getting another 2 hours of sleep is critical.

Once I'm well, I must make up for lost time. I spend the next three weeks catching up on life, even though I only missed two days of life. Somehow, these things compound. I'll work so hard to get things done, I'll wear myself out and get sick again. It's a vicious cycle that never ends.

The Wheel & The Grind

Over the years, my Uncle Paul's paint crew did numerous renovations to historic houses around northern Long Island. Huntington, as well as its surrounding areas, was well-tread by multiple presidents, politicians, and famous folks in music, movies and literature. The township is packed to the gills with 100-, 200-, and even a few 300-year-old houses – literal tinderboxes waiting to explode into crackling fireballs at the mere mention of the word matchstick.

We once painted a giant, three-story historical Victorian in wealthy Laurel Hollow where the paint melted off the house like icing off a hot cake until it stood as naked as a southern bell with her yellow ball gown around her ankles. Apparently, the chemicals used to remove the old coat of paint hadn't properly washed out, causing it to de-glove the new layer as well. Then, we painted it again.

Over many refurb jobs, we'd been tasked with using blowtorches to burn the lead paint off towering, suborn-as-a-

mule wooden columns; frustratingly detailed, filigree medal-
lions; and complicated, rage-inducing dental moldings. We lit
more roof-linings and facades on fire than most fire depart-
ments handle in a year. We were experts at re-glazing valuable, ancient stained-glass windows, most of them set into a
home's design before the War of 1812. We took more trips
to the hardware store for glass replacement than the British
took across the Atlantic to harass the new settlers. And we
removed, sanded, repainted and rehung enough storm shut-
ters to build a few dozen houses with the square footage they
encompassed.

After a while, we got ourselves a bit of a reputation,
which was shocking because we looked like nothing more
than a cluster of degenerate maniacs… like cartoons after in-
adequately handling an explosive device. I personally wore
the same pair of blue shorts four years in a row. I used them as
a rag, a napkin, and to check my car's oil levels. By year two
they looked like a Jackson Pollock painting and by year four,
they looked like Jackson Pollock's studio floor. Of course, no
one would see us till we got on the job site and by then it was
too late. My uncle Paul, AKA Nud, the face of the company,
would gain us access to the property, then open the monkey
cages. Paint fumes managed to hide our gin-soaked scent and
a perpetual hustle around the house kept anyone from truly
nailing down our appearance.

Generally, no one really seemed to care. The guys
chopping down a 1950 Mercury and revamping it into a
flame-emblazoned hot rod aren't dressed in wedding gowns,
and the boys who are refurbishing your massive 1850 Victorian doll house to historic specifications aren't dressed as

butlers. As long as we kept our greasy leers at the women to a minimum, and didn't crank the radio at rock concert-levels, we were pretty much left to our devices.

That is, until we walked in the door. That's when all hell would break loose.

In the Summer of 1992, we attacked one of our biggest refurb jobs. A large historical three-story brick Colonial in Upper Brookville, a wealthy enclave nestled tightly along Long Island's 'gold coast.' Originally, the home of President William Howard Taft's brother Henry, it had been purchased by writing agent Ralph and his young boyfriend Tim. The large home sat in the middle of a palatial piece of property that had waned in prominence from neglect. Although not on the water, it was something you pictured the Great Gatsby inhabiting, swirling a cocktail with his finger from the back deck as he contemplated lost loves and green lights.

About two weeks prior to that job, my uncle Nud's paint crew were all working on the afore-mentioned Victorian doll house that was commissioned by the town board historical society to be reconditioned. It was a restoration job of the most extreme sorts, and we took great pride in doing the job well. We'd redone the whole bloody place over the course of a year. Inside and out. We'd accidentally lit the place on fire, broken windows, knocked gutters off the house and killed plants. For an entire year. But, we were the best at restoration, and it would be a masterpiece.

At the end, the owners of the house had officially had enough of the painters. We were there in the mornings when they awoke, in the afternoons at lunchtime, in the evenings

when they came home, and on the weekends when they wanted to relax. The wife of the house had become completely
unnerved. Everywhere she turned, there was a painter. If she
looked out the window – a painter. If she went out onto the
porch for a drink – a painter. It got to the point where she was
looking under the bed before going to sleep to see if there was
a painter. To her, it was like a bad movie come horribly to life.

One morning Kevin found himself in the bathroom
just off the large open kitchen. Kevin had settled in to relieve
himself of all his internal waste when the entire family barged
into the kitchen for their morning breakfast. They happily
munched on toast and Cherrios and blabbed away about the
plans for the day. Kevin held tight hoping they'd leave so he
could finish his business in peace, but it was of no use. Kevin had been out the whole night before, and his grumbling
intestines were a whirlpool of beer bubble air and egg sandwich nitroglycerin. He leaned to the side in hopes of sneaking
some air out quietly, but the gas escaped in a blast, which re-
verberated inside the bowl and ricocheted around the country
kitchen like a gunshot. The clang of cereal bowls and spoons
quickly ceased. Little Suzie looked at Mom. Dad at Bobby.
The sounds of eyeballs whirling around the kitchen was deaf-
ening. Kevin couldn't wait any longer. He drained his colon
with a roar equal to a monster truck tractor pull. It took all
his strength to keep from yelling an orgasmic sigh of relief.
Suddenly, all the chairs squeaked across the kitchen floor. Dad
was late. Bobby had to go to work. Suzie was late for summer
school, and Mom just needed to get the hell out! Cereal bowls
hit the sink and feet shuffled across the tiles like a police raid.
The back door shut, car engines turned, and the gravel of the

driveway pelted against the side of the house like buckshot. Kevin waited a few minutes and returned to work.

It was not known who had fouled their bathroom that morning. It could have been any one of us. It didn't matter. It was the last straw. We'd fouled their bushes and gawked at their daughter. We'd lingered and crept for far too long. This was the kind of rude and intrusive behavior we'd displayed for over a year. That afternoon the owners took Nud to the side and pleaded for him to finish the job. Even if it meant cutting corners and doing the meticulously polished work we were so noted for.

Of our many infractions, beside the aforementioned crimes, was smoking weed in the little crow's nest atop the house, using said crow's nest as a napping spot, throwing knives from the crow's nest in distance/accuracy competitions, dancing on the roof, using the nearby woods as a dumping ground, smoking enough cigarettes to choke a city skyline, and generally taking over the front porch for our own lazy siestas.

It was an early May afternoon, and we had just dotted the i's and crossed the t's of the exterior. We decided to grab some beers and sit down by the docks and watch the boats pass in front of the sunset. Our buzz was growing steadily when a large boat pulled up to the docks. A voice rang out calling us to join them for a boat tie-up party in Long Island Sound.

The lure being that it was Cinco De Mayo.

Cinco de Mayo? We all looked at one another. What exactly is Cinco de Mayo? Do we celebrate Cinco de Mayo? Does it matter? We all gave a blood curdling party cry in unison. Some of us boarded the boat. Some of us dove into the water *then* boarded the boat. None of us remembers much after that.

Yes, fireworks were shot, and booze was guzzled, and there was a whole lot of Cinco De Mayo. We cruised out to Long Island Sound and tied up along an array of motor and sail boats of all shapes and sizes. A huge floating island of fiberglass and wood. We hopped from one boat to the other, drinking whatever was offered by the host of the ship. A frosty drink whirling in a blender here, an ice-cold beer there. We dove into the water to cool off and back onto another boat for some grass and hash.

Unfortunately, we missed work the next day. In fact, we were missing at sea for several days. When we returned with fresh baked skin and red eyes, we were all fired on the spot. My uncle told us that we would never work for him again. This day was known as "El dia de Muerte." The day of death. But, as the weeks went on, Nud continued to get work and now he was strapped for a crew.

My uncle was constantly getting work, and to turn it away in the spring and summer months was negligent. Winters can be lean, so you always take as many summer jobs as you can. Even if it means working nights or Saturdays. The crew had been fired and rehired countless times. The whole roster scrapped in one fell swoop, and back intact the following Monday.

At Laurel Hollow, we were again hired to refurbish the Taft house to its former glory, which meant stripping the place down and attacking it in bits and pieces… and the first order of business was to remove every single piece of metal and hardware from every door and wall fixture inside the home so we could get the antique muck removed and buffed to a shine. Every single doorknob, rosette, latch plate and hinge. Every handle, lock, screw and rail. Plus, all the little detailed doo-dads and do-hickies around the place like wall sconces, gas lamps, light switch plates, candleabras and butler bells. All of it documented, numbered and cataloged. It was, without a hint of exaggeration, a small mountain of metal.

Our workstation was the detached four-car garage where we kept paint, buckets, ladders and set up multiple sawhorse and plywood tables. Lashed to the end of a thick, sturdy workbench, one that William Taft himself could have sat upon, was an electric hand drill that we fitted with a disk buffer attachment. Its sole task, other than to drive everyone insane for its insistent whine, was to clean and shine all the metal we'd removed from the house. And that task went to… not me. Thank God. That brutal task went to Chris Campion who spent about six weeks, eight hours a day, grinding away at "the wheel" as we called it… usually pronounced in some kind of sea captains' drawl to indicate its prominence as Chris's bane of existence – his white whale. The wheel struck fear in his heart because it was an unending task, whose pain would be passed down to children through the ages as an example of a life gone astray when poor report cards were inevitably brought home from lollygagging dreamers. "Children, let me tell you about… THaaWhhheeeel."

Almost immediately, Chris knew his job was more like an imprisonment. Not even two hours into the task did he emerge from the garage, eyes bleary with tears, hearing almost completely shot, and his nerves rattled to the point of shaking. His only relief was a few minutes of sunshine, a cig-arette, and knowing in six short hours he'd be at a bar, tipping back cold beers so he could escape the misery of his plight.

The rest of us in comparison had it easy. Physically. Mentally was a different ball game. Those of us who entered and worked in the house were at the mercy of either Ralph or Tim, and at certain times, both. They were incredibly per-snickety. On top of us almost the minute we walked in the side door, they watched every swipe of the sandpaper, every stroke of the brush, and every ladder maneuver through the tight and complicated ancient halls designed for people half our size. When not asking questions, Ralph and Tim were telling us how to do our jobs – a component that ground the process to a halt. The new owners weren't going to let the inmates run the asylum, so they clamped down on us *immediately*.

Fastidious in their ways, Ralph and Tim insisted we carpool to the house to curtail traffic in their loose-stone driveway. Every morning, Me, Chris, Pat, and Jerry would pile into Fred's light blue two-door Oldsmobile Cutlass Su-preme, a car whose doors weighed more than today's cars weigh in total. We'd meet in town and stuff ourselves in the lush leather seats. The drive was 25 minutes, and by the time we got there, we'd be totally zonked on marijuana. I'd taken to rolling massive honker joints with cardboard filters on the end for powerful direct inhalations, something I learned in Jamaica. With the windows rolled up, we'd cut off the oxygen supply and convert Fred's Cutlass into a rolling opium den. Spilling out onto the driveway, the five of us looked as if we'd arrived in a clown car for a Bob Marley concert.

Early in out tenor, we began enjoying our lunch on

the Gatsbyesque back deck until we were informed that we weren't welcome there. We shifted to eating under the large weeping willow centered in the large yard until it was clear we didn't want to be seen *at all*. We began eating in the darked garage, sitting on five-gallon buckets, and even *that* was pushing it, so we had to filter through the garage's backdoor and eat behind the garage in a long narrow alcove littered with decades of discarded materials, up against a rusting metal fence dense with ivy and buzzing with insects. The alcove was a danger of unmarked barrels filled with toxic liquids, and ancient broken glass jutting out at random, flesh-slicing angles.

The job was pure madness, and not because we were blitzed on weed. It seemed every other day we were in a different part of the house, scrambling to accomplish some last-minute detail. Because this was a complete renovation, we were either just ahead of another crew doing prep work, or behind another crew doing cleanup. We had to sand something and stain it before the electricians or plumbers came, or clean and dust something that was being installed by burly men hauling in half a staircase, or drilling a 900-pound chandelier into the ceiling. After the crews left, we'd need to fill holes or paint unsightly scratches, seemingly doing errands best left to the end when everyone finished their job other than the painters.

One clear bright morning, as the sun was shining in through some skylights on a newly minted hallway, I heard Tim wail in agony down the corridor like he'd lost his toy poodle in a meat grinder. Apparently, the professional floor sanders let a newbie tackle the job of sanding the small, twisty staircase steps that lead to a third-floor library. The El Salvadorian misinterpreted his assignment and used a massive, industrial 20" disk floor sander on the steps instead of doing them by hand, gouging brutal, unsightly, half-moons deep into the 150-year-old hickory. Looking at it myself, I shuddered from the horror – a complete and total hack-job. It took Ralph and Tim weeks to fully recover, if they ever truly did. After that, the screws were tightened… literally and metaphorically. Their hovering became blanketing, their advice the law, and their timeline shrank from early Fall, to get the hell out ASAP.

It was essential to condense a year's worth of work into three months, and we were down to our last few weeks. It was all-hands-on-deck. We brought Kevin and Lug from another job to work in the largest crew we could form, and the madness grew as other workers marched through the door – electricians, carpenters, plumbers, and a small parade of fabulous interior designers.

Eventually we divided and conquered. We were allowed to finish bedrooms and halls in one swoop and move to another location. We were inside and out, up and down. Some rooms we weren't allowed to enter. Mainly the kitchen and two massive, lush, dark-wood sitting rooms, which looked as if they hadn't changed since Taft himself was president, essentially making them museum dioramas – velvety fabric lounging sofas, polished grand pianos, and fireplaces large enough to dance in. The couple's bedroom required the most attention as Tim wanted the complete bed, bath and dressing room of his dreams. That level of focus required the sacrifice of one member of our crew to tend to, and that delicate daily garden went to Fred.

Standing at six foot one with slicked-back, wavy blond hair and piercing blue eyes, Fred was the most calm and mysterious painter of our crew. Fred spoke softly, listened carefully, and moved with a calmness that belied his size. He was exactly what Hitler dreamed of in his sleep - the perfect button-nosed solider whom, when handed a task, did it immediately and looked positively Arian doing it. One day as I passed one of the two entrances to Ralph and Tim's bedroom, I saw Fred standing with his hands on his hips, talking to Tim who was out of sight. Passing the second entrance, I then saw Tim who was completely naked, having just gotten out of the shower, talking to Fred as if standing in a coffee shop chatting with a neighbor.

Ramping up the timeline, Chris persevered in the garage behind The Wheel – it's scream unabated as he pressed warm metal into the drill's spinning brush. As Chris became more exhausted and despondent, he'd easily lose focus – the wheel catching the edge of a lock plate, pin-balling it around the garage like a Chinese throwing star. On any given day, Chris could have lost his life as rusty metal shot across the interior, threatening to impale an artery or the temple of his head. Eventually his task bore fruit as the heavy wooden doors were reconstructed and placed on their hinges, glistening with fresh stains and paints, their hardware glowing like the edge of a knife.

At the end, the owners were so weary of us, they began to corral us like cattle. We weren't allowed to use the front door, the back door or wander through the main foyer. Our final task, done in the baking heat of the afternoon sun, was to burn, sand and paint the second-floor upper deck railing that jutted from the house's side over the sunroom below. We used a ladder to gain access from the outside, eliminating any need to traipse through the house – avoiding confrontation or naked encounters. The deck railing finials seemed endless, and the late August heat beat down on us like an oven. Our only relief was to take quick shade under the large weeping willow in the back, but that was continuously frowned upon. Our last refuge with a crew that size was to take breaks in the garage with the wheel. Fortunately, the wheel laid dormant, its job finished and Chris free from his Sisyphean task. He was now with us on the burning deck, wilting under the spotlight of earth's deadliest star. Although masked and goggled through the wheel's unforgiving process, at least Chris was shaded – the garage being a fairly cool and dark place to be. He immediately went from a cave-like setting to desert plains exposure. Out of the frying pan and into the fire.

During the last week of work, dashing towards the finish line, our welcome had worn more than the mangled hickory steps. It was pure mayhem. Ratcheting up the madness in the bubbling stew was the fact we were painting the trim (all 5,000 miles of it) in painfully slow drying oil, which filled the air with head-swimming toxic fumes, rendering everyone giddy and off-kilter, stacking onto it the fact we were all sunworn, drunk, and stoned to boot. At one point I was painting white, topcoat oil finish on the front door frame, while no more than five feet away a carpenter was spraying sawdust on me from his circular saw like one might blast a cloud of smoke from a motorcycle exhaust pipe. All while movers were hauling bedframes, lengthy couches, African statuettes, and rolled up rugs large enough to cover football fields. I was treated like nothing more than a ragdoll, and was reprimanded for exiting the front door, even though the 300-pound gorilla trying to place an antique grandfather clock in my standing spot, and was going to clock me if I didn't get the fuck out of the way, literally grabbed my shoulder and pushed me out the front door. I was then reprimanded, again, for smoking a cigarette outside the front door while watching landscapers plant dwarf pines which would no doubt be decorated with twinkling lights at Christmas. Then I was reprimanded, *again*, when I threw my cigarette butt in the bushes. It was a second-to-last defiant act before leaving, with our final rebellious act being a sprawling, unsightly picnic under the weeping willow and back deck, the likes which hadn't been seen since the massive Italian and French bacchanal paintings of the 1600s.

Like most animals, the longer you're penned, the more you need to break free. And like most painters, we began to grate on the owners much like the previous job where we were begged to finish and leave. Of our many infractions on this job, besides being an unruly crew of eight, including Nud, was spilling an entire can of paint on the floor; cracking an ancient window in the ancient kitchen door; breaking the ancient doorknob of said ancient kitchen door; throwing crushed beer cans down the rotting alley behind the garage; filling the flower beds with endless cigarette butts; playing the radio at 'rock concert' levels; talking too loudly; using the weeping willow for knife-throwing competitions; using the branches of said weeping willow to whip each other; and generally being a rowdy, uncouth, stumbling, bumbling crew of mischief and mayhem, that somehow possessed the golden touch of home restoration prowess.

Regrettably, I didn't see the final outcome because I went back to college. I saw enough to know it was an excellent job, but I can only assume it all came together perfectly and was met with praise. Another job well done. Firm handshakes all around.

It's possible it was featured in a local paper as a premiere example of a renovation done right like much of our past handiwork – an array of professional photos spotlighting the lush green bushes of the exterior, the interior showcasing the meticulous work done, especially the burnished brass that bejeweled the place. Maybe an inset shot of Henry Taft.

Only weeks before, the place was a near disaster, the floor carpeted with cigarette butts, drop clothes and scraps of wood... now, a feature in Better Homes and Gardens. Missing from the piece, of course, would be the paint crew. The rag tag experts behind the scenes and their unwashed shorts. The guys who made it all happen. Their crooked fingers, reddened eyes... their zonked, far-away stares.

Mind Over Matter

About two years before I met my wife, and two years after my nervous breakdown, I was walking the streets of Manhattan when I started to feel an incredibly sharp pain in my testicles. The first thing I thought was: OH MY GOD I HAVE TESTICULAR CANCER AND I'M GOING TO DIE! That's what normal, sane men think when they feel pain like this. I immediately did nothing about it. Because I'm a man who didn't have a primary care physician, nor any health insurance, I ignored it and hoped the pain would go away. Guess what? It didn't. So, I continued to walk the streets of Manhattan – work, partied, and even did the occasional trek to someplace outside of New York City – all with this nagging pain in my testicles.

I tried giving myself a testicular self-examination following a "how-to" diagram I found online, but I found it difficult to understand what I was feeling. Mainly because if you grab a testicle and really roll it round in your hand, squeeze it, and finger over its strange surface, you get the sense that there's all kinds of knots, tumors, and unusual growths happening. You *think* it's going to feel like a de-shelled hard-boiled egg in a thin supermarket produce bag, but it's more like a bulbous lollipop that fell on the floor of a kindergarten crafts room and jammed into a cold, wet sock. You juggle the nuts around and think, "What is that? A coat button? Gravel from the driveway? Twine used for bundling the cardboard recycling??? Then you think: HOLY SHIT THERE'S A SHITLOAD OF TUMORS ON MY TESTICALS! It's a completely normal reaction of a sane (paranoid) man who's just given himself a testicular self-exam.

I'm not a doctor, so I was unable to determine if what I was feeling was normal or deadly. The pain unfortunately continued. I continued to ignore it. Doesn't cancer go away if you ignore it? Same with heart disease, high cholesterol and many *many* other serious health issues?

The answer is no.

Eventually the pain got so bad I had to do something about it. I asked a few friends as well as my girlfriend Ali if they knew someone out in the world who could recommend a doctor who would do a full physical exam for a cut-rate fee. Sort of like negotiating an oil change on your car, or the best price on a hotel room. Nothing came of the search.

Finally, Ali had a workmate who knew a doctor who would do an exam at a decent price, no health insurance required. I went into the exam completely blind, not knowing anything about this doctor. Nothing. No credentials, no medical history. No knowledge of their residency or if they did a fellowship. I didn't know if they interned or if they even spoke English. What choice did I have? I was practically a beggar in the street asking for pocket change.

"Anyone spare an extra testicular exam?"

For all I knew, this "doctor" could have been the local butcher, a parrot trainer, or a world-champion yodeler.

On a cloudy, yet warm, Fall Sunday morning, I met this doctor at an office on the upper west side near Columbus circle. When I stepped inside the office building lobby, it was virtually empty. It was Sunday and the fires of industry had stopped churning for the day. I took a lonely elevator ride to a darkened floor, to an office where I met my doctor for the first time. Standing confused in the un-lit waiting room, I spun around until one of several unmarked wooden doors opened and I was greeted by a Hasidic Jew around the age of 55. With his distinguished salt and pepper beard, wide-brimmed black fedora hat, and boxy black over coat, he waved me in with not much more than a simple hello.

I followed him into the large room, which was essentially one giant examination room filled with cold, aging equipment about 20 years past their prime. The view was excellent, overlooking the west side of Central Park and the rest of New York's eastern board.

Although a bright day, Dr. Schechter never flipped on the lights, keeping the room mysteriously grey. I got the feeling it wasn't his office; like he was using it temporarily in-between bouts of serial killing and butchering.

"Please undress and I will start the exam."

The doctor exited the room, and I slipped on a typical frontal robe that tied in the back. Upon entering, he came to the black leather exam table and gave it a smack.

"Sit."

I hopped on the table, and he took my vital signs, which all seemed normal.

"Lie here on your side."

Within seconds he had his fingers in my ass, examining my colon, my prostate, and whatever else was within arm's reach. The exam was thorough, and I was generally not disappointed in his overall scope of work. He examined my testicles, pushed my stomach, poked my intestines, pressed my lower abdomen, squeezed my kidneys, knocked on my spine, pressed my neck, and handled just about every organ, bone, or pipe that may be associated with the testicles in any way, shape or form.

After the exam, I dressed and sat at the large wooden desk, facing the window as the drab day grew brighter, but not any less grayer. Eventually, the doctor sat on the other side of the desk, opened drawers, and fished around for another pen, solidifying my thoughts about the office not really being his. He sat quietly writing things on a yellow legal pad, noting things he'd written, cross-referenced other things he'd written, then contemplated everything as a whole. He wrinkled his brow, shrugged his shoulders, and at one point seemed to argue silently with what he'd written, like the legal pad was another combative physician in the room who'd come to debate his notes. It was clear the doctor was stumped.

After the longest three minutes of my life, the doctor shook his head, pinned his shoulders up under his ears, opened his mouth and said, "Have you considered that you're channeling your nervous energy into your testicles?"

The information hit me like a bucket of water, and just like that, the testicular pain went away. A weight *lifting* off me.

That was it.

I was channeling all my nervous energy into my testicles.

He was 100% correct.

I went in for a physical exam and got a phycological exam.

I nodded and said, "Yes, I think you could be right."

He nodded as well.

"You should try meditation and exercise."

"That's a good idea. I will." I said.

At that point, the relief from the testicular pain was so lightening, the doctor could have suggested Vogue dancing, and I would have agreed to it being an excellent therapeutic treatment for pain.

I gave the doctor $100 cash, and left the office with a gentle pat on the back as he closed the door quickly behind me.

The sharp testicular pain never fully returned. I joined a gym around the corner that offered a special rate if I trained during non-peak hours – 7pm until they closed at 11pm.

A dull testicular pain would return occasionally, but when it did, I knew I was channeling stress into my groin. I eventually learned to reroute the nervous energy somewhere else less painful and less important – like my kidneys, brain, and heart.

Watch Your Mouth

My wife Rita has been known to mangle the English language. Massacre it. Slice it up and glue it back together like a ransom note.

Phrasings have come out in so many funny and disturbing ways, that it can leave you in awe. Like a good firework show.

Just the other day she told me Max was "upstairs eating penis." I dropped the mug I was washing in the sink, turned in her direction, and watched her shake a mound of Planters dry-roasted nuts into her hand and catapult them into her mouth. What Max does with his life is up to him… but that's when he's an adult. Right now, he's 13, and I don't want him eating any nuts other than Planters. Maybe Blue Diamonds almonds, but those can be extremely salty.

I reminded her to emphasize the T in peanuts and she replied with a few practice "peanuTs" while putting the nut jar back in the cabinet.

"peanuTs"

"peanuTs"

"peanuTs"

Occasionally, she and I practice emphasizing together, the two of us standing face-to-face, spitting difficult English words back and forth in a spittle volley. It's hard for Rita (and many others) to say certain English words because her tongue is not trained to unusual mouth placements… the tongue pressed against the roof of the mouth… the hard R, especially when it's followed by an L, as in Girl… and many S words, especially when a tricky consonant follows, like a W. Listening to Rita say SWIRL, is like listening to someone sing the Alphabet Song while attempting to tie a cherry stem into a knot with their tongue.

Last year at my parent's country club for a Fourth of July celebration, Rita let another mangulage fly. Mind you, this is a categorically conservative crowd. It takes a least nine or 10 vodka tonics to get these people to drop their guard, and even when they do, it comes out in strange and uptight ways.

Max and his buddy Arthur were done with the school year, and talk of Junior high was already on the tongue. Max was confessing his nervousness about a new school. After the four parents divulged a healthy dose of wise words, Rita capped the philosophical advice with a good-hearted, "You've got to fuck!"

Well, let me tell you *that* pricked up a few ears, especially since we were right outside the food tent where lines of people in expensive clothes were piling their plates. The WASPy wives of dermatologists shepherding their brood through a queue of steaming hotdogs, don't like foreigners encouraging their young sons to fuck at their new school. Especially at that age.

"FocUS," I said to Rita, "They've got to FOC-US."

After a good group laugh, Rita again made the effort to add the "us" after her Brazillian accented "foc" – giving it a few practice tries.

"FocUS"

"FocUS"

"FocUS"

Something I've always found slightly amusing is that some South Americans and Europeans say, "wash your teeth" in reference to brushing the teeth. For me it sounds as if the teeth are yanked from the face like dentures and scrubbed like laundry on a washboard.

The Brazillians don't have the "TH" sound in their vocabulary as in BooTH or THink, so when Rita tries to plant her tongue under her upper front teeth to make the sound, it becomes a sputtering Daffy Duck impression. Her tongue either flaps like a flag in the wind, or gets lost in the mouth and whistles like a teakettle.

Needless to say, when Rita first told Max to, "wash your tits" I wasn't sure where she was going with the advice. Sure, everyone should wash *everywhere*, but being the skinny boy of seven that he was, the advice fell flat.

"Brush his teeTH" I told her – and really punched the "TH" at the end.

Rita proceeded to show me her teeth like a neighing horse, planting her tongue, and give me a series of practice "ttthhhhs." They didn't quite work so I did the same with my mouth and we sat facing each other going "tttthhhh" like two snakes fighting over a scorpion.

"TeeTH"

"TeeTH"

"TeeTH"

There's also the singular Tooth as well. My "tooth hurts" become my "toot hurts." Occasionally she doesn't even add a T at the end and will say my, "too hurts" or accidentally say my "my toe hurts" and I look down at her foot even though she's holding her face. I'll ask her, "how'd that happen?" and she'll reply that she bit down too hard on something, and I'll wonder why she bit her toe.

And I won't even get into the confusion she brings by swapping toes with fingers. She'll tell you she hurt her finger and is pointing towards the floor, and before you know it, we're deep into Abbott and Costello's *Who's on First* routine.

Our household is in a constant series of misunderstandings that would rival the verbal shenanigans of any half-hour television sitcom. On these comedy shows, someone misinterprets something and before you know it, the show's running gag is about trying to fix the issue caused by someone over-hearing something incorrectly. This is our life almost daily.

"Where's the rock?" Rita will ask, and I'll wonder why she needs a rock.

"What rock?" I ask. I get nervous because maybe there's some rock we use for everything. One we use as a doorstop, one we use as a hammer, and one we use as a just a rock – even though I can't think of any rock in the house at all.

"For the clothes to dry outside."

"Oh, the rack!" I say, "it's in the basement. I'll get it

out."

The other day on a walk, Rita asked me if Max does "Gratamattack" in school. "Gratamattck?" I ask, contorting my face into a fist. Is that a Marshal Art?

"Cindy says Nicoli is having trouble with Matt."

"Matt? Who's Matt?"

When all was said and done, there's no kid named Matt at all. There's no trouble or self-defense needed. Nicoli is not battling Matt, but math. Gratamattck is Rita's attempt to say Arithmatic. She took a crack at a difficult word and failed. Truthfully, I couldn't tell you what Arithmetic was in Portuguese if my life depended on it. So, I can't blame her.

A question to a friend will start a routine something like: "Do you like crazies?"

"Crazies… as in people?"

"No, in your potato salad."

"I'm sorry, what's a crazy? Is that food?"

"It's the little ting," she says, looking at the ceiling, her frustration boiling into a giggle. "Tiny dry grapes."

"Oh, raisins!"

"Yes, Raisins."

"Oh, yes. I love raisins."

Let's not get into the subject of putting raisins in potato salad.

And this silly exchange while going to the grocery store.

"Buy Moo Shoes."

"Moo Shoes? Is that in the dairy section?"

Long story short, it's mushrooms.

But the verbal shenanigans march in a never-ending parade and rear their ugly head when least expected. After my son suffered a terrible bought of Salmonella, Rita told everyone that the doctor at the children's hospital "really knew what he was doing" and "he was an idiot." When people wrinkled their brow and wondered why he was so competent, yet not intelligent, I had to explain to Rita and those listening to that Dr. Khan was an *Indian*, not an idiot.

But the language issues go both ways. During a bar-b-que in Brazil with many of Rita's family in attendance, I apparently called someone at the table a derogatory term for a well-used vagina. Then there was the time I was talking to Rita's brother-in-law Antonio (God rest his soul), the patriarch of the family, and told him that American's "likes to fuck." I can't even begin to tell you what I said that got me to that point, but let me assure you Antonio threated me (through Rita) that if I came back without knowing better Portuguese, he'd be very disappointed. Apparently, I have an excellent knowledge of Portuguese curse words without knowing it.

When Rita and I were first dating, I wanted to know if she wanted a cocktail with vodka, which she found incredibly confusing because *vodka* is essentially the word *cow* in Portuguese. Why would anyone drink cow? "Is it milk?" she thought. Why would adults drink milk at a bar?

My personal favorite came in the form of sunscreen. Rita, being concerned about the ingredients in the sunscreen asked me if it was safe for our young son Max to wear. I assured her it was, because it was free of Parabens. She looked at me confused, nodded and walked away. We never discussed it again. Later I learned that Parabéns means *congratulations* in Portuguese. So, the lotion we used was safe and free from congratulations. I learned this when my birthday came in the Fall and her family flooded my Facebook timeline with multiple *Parabéns!* which in this form, essentially means *Happy Birthday!*

The list of verbal infractions is virtually endless and don't always come from the mouth.

Grocery lists I've scanned have items like "Han Soup," which I'm sure is a delicacy somewhere, but not in America. It forces me to play word scramble games. Does Rita mean Hand Soap or is it a can of soup that I can't seem to unravel. I go to the soup section and scan the soups. There's no Ham soup, but could hand be something she's misheard over time? I can't think of a meat other than ham that rhymes with *han*, but is it a brand? Hammonds or something like that? Chunky seems to have all kinds of tantalizing flavors like chicken tortilla and hearty creamy chicken bacon carbonara. None of which sounds like *han*. Sometimes I'll get deep into Rita's head and speak in her Brazilian accent, like a method actor, and channel her and how she misinterpreted the word han… or soup… people walk away nervously because the six-foot tall blonde Brazilian is speaking to the soups on the shelf. All of this solvable with a text to ask her about what Han Soup might be.

Turns out it was hand soap.

The Brazilians in their beautiful and frustrating ways have taken certain words and made them their own.

For example:

Prosciutto. In every country on the planet, prosciutto is an air-dried, salty ham, but in Brazil, it's cheap boiled ham. Not a big deal, but Rita was cooking a dish one evening and asked for a pound of prosciutto. I went and procured a pound of prosciutto, which cost me 40 bucks, when all she wanted was about four dollars of cheap ham most butchers toss on the floor.

Flan, the creamy milk desert most associated with Mexico, with drippy caramel top, is called pudding in Brazil. I tell people Rita is bringing pudding as a dessert to a dinner party, and they're usually perplexed because NO ONE brings pudding for dessert, but are pleasantly surprised when she walks in the door with a mouth-watering flan.

And I don't even want to get started on swapping of DO and MAKE.

I'm going to make the laundry

I'm going to do the dinner.

I'm going to make my eyebrows

In certain situations, it becomes downright tantalizing.

"I'm going to DO something special for your birtday."

I rub my hands together at the infinite possibilities, only to be presented with pudding.

The list goes on and on. Sheets have been called shits, and she's introduced me to people as her *has-been* (husband), which is actually true, in both cases.

Some of this is my fault. The reason being is I find my wife's misusage of the English language cute. When I watched movies as a kid and saw the beautiful foreign woman saying things incorrectly, it made me fall in love with her more. Same with my wife. The more things she says incorrectly, the more I swoon. Unfortunately, when I finally correct her, usually after a few years of saying something incorrectly, she gets mad at me.

"Why didn you tell me?!"

I don't blame her.

•••

Where my wife's language issues stem from a language barrier, my son's language issues stem from his inability to move beyond the literal word.

This, of course, is also my fault.

Being a writer, I tend to add flourish to what is happening in my life… adding color… painting a picture using words or exaggerations. Max doesn't get any of it. If I say something is a "million miles away" he asks if it's *actually* a million miles away. Yet if I say something is millions of miles away, like Mars from Earth, he'll ask: "is it really a million miles or is it like 100?" It seems my metaphors and my facts have confused him to no end.

In my family we have a large number of artists and scientists. I'm of the art variety, but my son got the scientist portion of the genes. He's brilliant in science, but doesn't seem to grasp the artistic aspects of things – especially those of the written word or what one might call metaphors… as well as similes, analogies and allegories. He seems unable to differentiate *embellishment* from *fact*, how one might *feel* in comparison to what is actually *happening*, and an artistic interpretation of events compared the hard, photographic evidence of what it is.

> Take for example this exchange from a few years ago.
>
> Me: Man, that sunshine really lifted me up.
>
> Max: Did the sun actually lift you into the air?

He's was being serious. His brow wrinkled and he was generally curious if this type of thing is capable of happening. Again, even though he's born of the science side of our family, and knows how gravity, sunshine, and almost everything *physically* works in the universe, he still asked me this stunning question. It's also an age thing. He doesn't yet know the sun doesn't make people defy gravity.

> Me: No, not literally. It was a metaphor.
>
> Max: What's literally mean?
>
> Me: It means of the literal word. It's exact meaning.
>
> Max: What's a metaphor?
>
> Me: It's sort of an artistic representation of what is happening and not literal.
>
> Max: Oh.

I don't know if he understood.

Perhaps that is my fault. Perhaps I started him on similes and comparisons when what he really needed was cold, hard facts. But it seems I'm incapable of doing so. To me, a trip to the store across town is "going to take forever" and after a long hard day, "my feet are killing me."

Still, he knows Mars is not 100 miles from earth. The kid is in advanced science classes. He's now 14, but I fear he's still capable of being lured into an unmarked van with a lollipop.

My wife suffers from the same issue.

Stating to Rita that something is "going to take for-ever" is met with her stone response of "It will only take an hour." What she doesn't realize is that an hour *is* forever in relation to the task at hand. She's very unreasonable (see: rea-sonable) and incapable of seeing the daunting nature of the task. An hour of scraping dog shit does take forever in my eyes, but an hour of eating potato chips is a chore that will only take seconds.

Then, I have to deal with both of them simultaneous-ly.

There's been a few times (often) where I'll be driving the car, boisterously telling a story with meticulous tidbits – adding dollops of those damn metaphors, similes and com-parisons, and turn to see my family blinking at me like two confused owls staring at a crying goat. I'll ask, "know what I mean?" even though I know the answer (it's no), and I'll need to repeat the story with none of the embellishments, difficult words, or accoutrements that made the story worth hearing in the first place. By the time I'm finished, I've re-told half the story in a way that would put most listeners to sleep.

It's a constant clash between the presenter and the presentation. Like asking Shakespeare to use a Power Point presentation to get his point across.

Because of this, I tend to give basic details verbal-ly, and leave my regaling to the written word. That's a prob-lem because I find I'm having full-blown conversations with myself. The other day, my wife came into the bathroom as I stepped out of the shower, and I was silently talking to myself – mouth moving with enthusiastic animation, but nothing coming out.

"What are you saying?" she giggled.

"Nothing," I said slightly embarrassed.

I have conversations with myself about what I'm going to write, and that tends to come out in strange ways. Sometimes it comes out verbally with under-the-breath mumbles, and sometimes it comes out with contorted facial expressions, which may be worse than the mumbling. watching someone on the streets of New York mumbling to themselves is common. These days, it's usually someone speaking on the phone via earbuds. When it's someone talking to the voices in their head, it seems alarming, but nothing too unusual. When I speak to myself and no words come out, the conversation is displayed with contorted facial expressions that can be mis-construed as a heart-attack, face-melting acid freak-out, or appendicitis. I can't tell you the number of times my wife has entered the kitchen to find me knee-deep in a silent conversa-tion with myself, my facial expression of anger, followed by an array of reactions that range from head-shaking disappoint-ment, to shoulder-shrugging apathy – performances so gro-tesque and diverse it would put a tenacious troop of improv actors to shame. My calling as a silent film actor coming 100 years too late.

But this embarrassment can't send me inward. I must continue to have outward conversations with myself, mouth moving like that silent movie star, or I end up standing around somewhere looking angry, head veins bulging from my tem-ples because I'm containing a full conversation inside my head without moving my lips.

There's no winning. I either look like a man about to shit his pants, or one of the many psychos among us who are talking to themselves. There comes a point in which you don't care what others think… about your mouth moving silently, or if you're saying things incorrectly.

The only thing to do is go for it. Talk it out. Say what you need say. Even if you freak people out standing around you, or you call someone a well-used cow.

Hellllooooo in There

It was 2:00am and I was sitting in the doctor's office with a nosebleed that wouldn't stop. I was seven or eight years old at the time and the incessant bleeding forced my mother to call Dr. Gilbert in a panic, who lived down the street from us. His office was attached to his house, and it reminded me of my grandmother's living room. Walnut wood paneling with green fabric couches in the waiting room, and buzzy overhead lighting dim enough to project a film.

Dr. Gilbert wasn't happy about being awoken so early for an emergency. Most 78 year-old doctors aren't. Dr. Gilbert was a miserable man to begin with. A pediatrician with the bedside manner of a flamethrower. He annually checked me for a hernia by clutching my testicles with ice-cold hands and squeezing them like a vice. When I'd inevitably scream, "ow," his response was, "Oh, stop it, you big baby!" He was gruff and nasty, and I actually hated him, but he was our family pediatrician and if we needed to literally run to his house, we could.

My sister hated him too. I don't think anyone liked him. His head was like an unsplit firewood log, and his mouth was set in a perpetual frown. One time we saw him in the pharmacy, also literally down the street from us, and when I said hello, he looked down on me like a street urchin begging for change. Honestly, I could never understand why he chose the pediatric profession. I believe he hated kids… his own included. Maybe he had gambling debts because he practiced almost until his death. I would chalk up the dedication to the Hypocritic Oath, or a dutiful honor to the health and safety of the children in the community, but as far as I could tell, he wanted us all dead.

It was the middle of a freezing cold winter during this particular bloody nose. Sitting in his icy office, under an icy gaze, Dr. Gilbert yanked my face up to look inside my nostril. My mother tried to stop the bleeding with Vaseline, something a boxing cut-man knows all too well. But Doc Gilbert wasn't happy with the nasal gunk. He grabbed a wad of tissues and plugged his giant carrot finger up my nose to swab it all out. My head nearly popped off my neck.

He informed my mother that the vein needed to be cauterized. Burned closed. Chemically. That news didn't go over too well with me, but I knew if we didn't slam the thing shut, I'd bleed to death in his mid-century modern office. Dr. Gilbert cupped his hand on top of my head like one might clamp a rusty outdoor faucet, and jammed a cotton-swabbed stick so far up my nose, I believe it erased the memory of the entire second grade. My jaw tightened and teeth clenched as the searing of the chemical burn wafted into my sinuses, locking me in frigid pain. I tried to escape, but Doc Gilbert's firm grip locked me in place.

"That should do it," he growled and tossed the swab into the trash.

After that, I felt like a ragdoll. My mother zipped up my thick jacket, yanked me off the table and took me home.

It's one of the many dramatic bloody noses I've had over the years. Some of them more memorable than others. Any wild, un-caught kickball to the face, any errant elbow in a dog pile scrum, or even just a gentle breeze to the bridge of my nose would get a nosebleed going.

Usually, the cold weather was to blame. The cold, raw air would crust my fragile nasal cavity into a cave of crumbling plaster. When I was nine, my father and I, along with our family friends the Lawrences, went hiking along the Appalachian trail. During a particularly cold night, sleeping in a house that wasn't winterized, I awoke to a nosebleed that wouldn't quit. Within minutes, the entire group was tending to my nose… everyone chiming in with a slew of nosebleed triage skills.

"Lean your head forward."

"Put your head back."

"Don't put your head back!"

"Pinch the top of your nose."

"Put ice on it."

"Don't swallow the blood."

All of these nuggets of medical advice useful to some degree.

Being the fairly rambunctious child I was, I was constantly knocking my nose. Yes, stray balls and elbows, but just about anything would start a stream. The tension surface of pool water, a miscalculated frisbee catch, knocking heads with others in a football pile, and of course, a particularly strong sneeze.

A bout of sneezing could easily get a nosebleed going. I'd blow my nose and was presented a horror show in a tissue filled with blood… enough to attract every vampire up and down the coast. By the time the nose bleeds subsided, my allergies took over. When I wasn't holding clumps of tissues to my face to dam bleeding, I was holding clumps of tissues to dam the mucous. I became one of those kids who carried a little plastic tissue pack around, one of the seven signs of clichéd nerdiness along with tape-mended eyeglasses, pen-packed pocket protectors, and a proclivity to wear bowties.

I was allergic to about 150 different things. Just about anything would set off a sneezing attack: fresh-cut grass, hay, mold, mildew, a cloud of baking powder, pepper, dry air, saw dust, pollen, ragweed, dogs, cats, photos of dogs and cats, dust and especially their pilots: dust mites. Have you seen a magnified photo of a dust mite? They look like mutant crabs… something from a sci-fi/horror film in which the crab creature enters the skull and latches its gnarly fangs into the brain stem, taking over the mind and transforming its host into a mindless killer. It's terrifying.

My sinuses were either swollen shut or hollow, cavernous shells. I believe if I'd lived a life allergy-free, my nose would be rather slim and shapely. But a lifetime of honking, blowing, twisting and digging has made it a bulbous ball of clay. It's never been busted or broken, but yank any nose to the left and right a few million times and it's bound to lose its shape.

The head is a strange and mysterious place. I'm very attached to mine. We have ear, nose and throat doctors and surgeons who can crack your noggin open like a coconut and look around, but for the most part, we really don't know what going on in there. Science fiction movies like *Fantastic Voyage* and *Innerspace* depict scenarios where rag-tag crew of scientists are shrunken to the size of tardigrades and injected into the body so they can poke around. We haven't developed that type of technology yet… at least I don't think we have. I'm sure there are those who *think* we have that technology – conspiracy theorists who are convinced the COVID-19 shot injected microphones, mind control devices, and miniature panels of philosophers bent on controlling the mind of the person they occupy.

But the body and the head can vary greatly from one person to the next. I can be standing next to someone who's unaffected by a cloud of dry grass blowing in their face, while a mold spore that travelled a country mile can set me off on a raging bout of sneezing that won't dissipate for days.

People… meaning anyone who's ever sneezed, or has seen someone sneeze, always have a slew of advice for allergies too.

"Have you tried Zyrtec?"

"What about Claritin?"

"Raw honey is good. Should be local though!"

"Have you tried those Neti pots?"

"Don't put flowers in the house."

"Don't have flowers outside the house!"

"Have you considered allergy shots?"

In my teens, I received heaping doses of allergy shots,

which alleviated all my allergies, and kept my head clear and dry for years. No issues arose in my nose from bleeding, or with mucous, other than the occasional sneezing attack.

Until I reached the age of 37.

At 37 it wasn't nosebleeds or endless allergies, but brain-splitting headaches. But not migraines. No. Nothing that pleasant. Cluster headaches. They come much less often than the average migraine, but what they lack in frequency they make up for in pain. Deemed "the suicide headache," it's been known to drive those who get them to take their own life. I've been fortunate to not get them frequently enough to drive me to self-inflicted death, but I can see why it garnered the name. When people ask me what they feel like, I can only describe it as: someone pushing their fist up through my sinuses, through my brain, and poking my right eyeball out with their finger. Fun!

Not surprisingly, at least for me, was the fact it was hereditary. My father was lucky enough to get these cluster headaches as well. I remember as a kid, entering the living room to find him writhing on the ground, moaning in agony like a man cleaning his system of heroin… while also having been shot in the eye. In my wildest dreams I could never imagine how bad they could be and in truth, I thought he was exaggerating. Whoops! Perhaps that was my punishment for being a disbeliever.

My father describes the pain as being poked in the eye with a red-hot poker. Others have described it with various descriptors – burning, pressure, stabbing, PAIN. Anything you could think of and more. Unfortunately, no one knows how these start or how to get rid of them. Scientists (normal-sized and not shrunken) think it's the usual suspects of stress, nerves and even alcohol intake. But none of those diagnoses is proven – at all. I think it's absolutely NOT alcohol intake, because I refuse to curb my alcohol intake. So, I blame it on stress. There are websites packed with info on how to treat the cluster headache, but everyone is different. Again, the experts like to weigh in.

"Have you tried meditation?"

"I like to hyperventilate."

"Does Tylenol work?"

"How about Advil?"

"Pure oxygen is the only thing that helps."

"Have you tried Ryzothypan?"

"What about a massage?"

"Have you tried a guillotine?"

In reality, there's not much you can do for a cluster headache other than bear it. I began taking Ryothypan, a quick-acting pill that melts on the tongue, but the effects were mixed, occasionally working and other times not. Like a medical round of Russian Roulette. Fortunately, these headaches come so infrequently, they don't really affect my life much at all.

The wear and tear my poor head has gone through over the years is quite amazing. I didn't take blows to the head like a boxer (although I did take a few pops here and there), but small incremental shocks take their toll over time. Can sneezing make you brain dead? I've sneezed so hard I've knocked my spine out of alignment, given myself whiplash, and pulled a muscle in my rib. How can the brain go unscathed from such brutal force? I've bled from my nose so many times, I could have supplied a blood bank. I've had headaches so bad the only way to escape the pain was to have an out of body experience.

My wife says I have a terrible sense of smell, and that's true, but Rita has a superhuman sense of smell. She can smell the future. She knows when food has gone bad before she sees it. She may be one of those people that can smell cancer or illnesses. I've considered finding her a job as a perfumer – those witches who mix flower extracts, wood drippings, and orange peel oils into elixirs. I can jam an onion up my nose and find it takes a solid 10 seconds to detect its pungent stench. Maybe that's a result of my nose's endless abuse. The deadening of my sinuses, the dulling of the brain. The years of headaches, nosebleeds, allergies, and endless sneezing, along with a constant rinse and blow cycle may have contributed some form of trauma. The amount of pressure my head and neck have endured may have affected my spine and skull in ways I'll never know. One day I could be on top of the world, and next thing I know, I've sneezed and forgotten five years of my life.

But as I've learned as I've walked through life's fickle little path – things can always get worse.

•••

The first time it hit me was during one of my son's Boy Scout ceremonies where the kids' received merit badges in front of crowd of a hundred people or so. The leaders announced each Scout's name and their awards… like 'wilderness survival' and 'first aid' and I shouted "Ow! Fuck!"

like someone with Tourette's Syndrome. I thought a pack of bees had swarmed my face and stung me, but when I touched my temple, nothing was there. Fortunately, I was in the back row and quickly fled the room, hoping the Scouts with newly minted expertise in first aid would run to help me, but only my friend Stephen followed, wondering what the hell happened to me. He examined my face, but nothing was wrong, other than my looks, which is debatable if there's a problem or not.

That Spring of 2023, at the tender age of 51, it seemed I'd arrived at the fourth stage of Noggin' Annoyances.

Electric shocks across my face.

They literally felt like I was being electrocuted – zapped with a cattle prod. Another delightful head experience in a long line of them. Besides the absolutely horrifying pain, was the fact that they came completely out of nowhere, without warning.

I vowed to see a doctor *immediately*.

One month and four attacks later, one of those attacks being at Disney World where I shouted around small children like a man receiving a hot poker up his ass, I finally went to my general practitioner, Dr. Stroman.

I was positive the good doctor would have multiple forms of advice and treatments for taking care of these lightning bolt pains.

"I can prescribe hard drugs."

"You need back and neck massages hourly."

"Take long baths in hot water."

"Refrain from exercise, work, or even moving."

That would have been the *preferred* explanation. Unfortunately, he couldn't do anything because I needed to see a "specialist." He diagnosed nerve pain, possibly some kind of facial neuralgia, and sent me to a neurologist 45 minutes away. Regrettably, I did not take immediate action and waited six months before *another* series of attacks rendered me fragile and worried. The referral to see a specialist expired, so I had to visit Dr. Stroman *again*. Like many people, I dislike going to the doctor, but waiting too long to do the right thing, forcing me to see the doctor more than was necessary, was an example of apathy coming back to bite me in the ass. Or in this case, the face.

A few weeks later, I met with Dr. Faresh, a neurologist who resembled Benjamin Franklin with a slightly better haircut and more importantly, better access to advanced medical information and technology. The office was packed with people who seemed to be in various stages of misery, like most medical offices, because we don't visit the doctor when healthy… especially neurologists. Accordingly, these patients seemed a few levels more miserable than your average waiting room victim, me being part of their unenvious group. They all were being self-electrocuted, suffering from acute or chronic pain, and ready to grab the nearest hatchet to axe their heads open to care for the problem themselves.

My sister-in-law Vivian, who suffered from a series of health issues, including cancer, was plagued by Bell's Palsy, which set off a terrible case of facial neuralgia. She told my wife Rita that it was a *10 out of 10* on the pain scale and she felt like dying. My wife knew from past colds and flus that my bitching and moaning was a 10 out of 10 on the *annoying* scale, when in *reality*, I was suffering *maybe* a 4 out of 10 on the pain threshold. Now that she had hard confirmation about the neuralgia pain from a woman who shared her bloodline, she knew I really was suffering this time around… even though *my* pain was a 12 out of 10… as most men would attest to.

After I explained my symptoms, Ben Franklin did all the tests required to get a general idea about my condition. He whacked my knees with one of those little rubber mallets, brushed my face and neck gently with the back of his hand, and made me look at his finger as he moved it in various directions.

I passed with flying colors.

I would say he was flirting with me, but he looked as though he wanted to get the hell out of there to do anything besides be a doctor. He then informed me that there was nothing *he* could do, and that I needed to see a neurological *specialist*. I thought he *was* the neurological specialist, but apparently not. I'm not sure how many levels deep these specialists go – perhaps deeper than video game boss levels. Franklin was a *general* neurologist, and I suppose he had just as much knowledge of the foot as he did the head. Brushing a foot with the back of the hand and showing it your finger as you move it around seems more like a fetish than anything, but I'm not a doctor. He prescribed an anti-seizure medicine that also worked as a nerve blocker called Oxcarbazepine – a mouthful of a word if I ever heard one. Oxcarbazepine. Rolls right off the tongue. Sounds like a series of words one would say to activate a sleeper agent deep inside enemy territory. Ox - Car - Baze - A - Pine.

Doctor Franklin/Faresh recommended I see a neurological specialist named Dr. Patoni, who fortunately for me was only five minutes from my house. A few days later, I went to see her. Dr. Patoni was very nice, and her hair was leagues better than Ben Franklin's. She was incurably informative too. Dr. Patoni was a migraine and head specialist. She didn't stroke my cheeks or hammer me like Dr. Faresh did *physically*, but she did make me look at her finger as it roamed around the office like a bumble bee. I believe they do this test for fun. She then asked a series of questions about what triggers my pain.

"Does it hurt when you exercise?"
"Does it hurt when you eat something cold?
"Does it hurt when you eat something hot?"
"Does it hurt when you're stressed?
"Does it hurt when a strong wind blows?"
"Does it hurt when you are sleeping"
"Does it hurt when you're awake?"
"Does it hurt if you've been bad or good?"

I believe I said *yes* to some of these, but really: "It's just kind of random."

She then diagnosed me with Trigeminal Neuralgia, aptly named because there are three nerves running through the right side of the face that hub at the back of the skull. One goes past the temple and over the eye across the forehead; one runs across the right cheek under the eye, the third through the jaw. All these nerves have little offshoots that finger up and down into the eye, teeth, ear, etc. Dr. Pantoni showed me a facial nerve chart on her iPad, then answered all 25 of my questions.

I asked her how to cure Trigeminal Neuralgia, and what the next steps would be. She said there was nothing *she* could do, because I needed to see… a *neurosurgeon.* SUR-GERY! That was something I didn't think I'd hear. She recommended I establish a relationship with a surgeon so I felt comfortable with them, and could plan surgery when I was ready, and hopefully *before* the pain progressed to emergency levels – in this case, not stopping *at all.*

She recommended her colleague Dr. Ricken, who was right around the corner from her, and, coincidentally, a few office doors down from Dr. Stroman.

I drove over half of long Island for appointments, when all I had to do was walk a few feet down the hall… go figure. Kind of like a treasure hunter who follows a map around the globe when they've been sitting on the gold the entire time.

Again, for some stupid reason, I waited six months to make an appointment. If you ignore these things, they simply go away. If you never have your cholesterol checked, it's probably perfect, and if the sharp pain in your chest comes and goes, it's probably gas or something. At the hedging of my wife, I made an appointment.

Before I could see Dr. Rickins, his assistant Debra had me get an MRI. That's when they stuff you inside one of those giant plastic imaging tubes that takes numerous pictures of your body. In my case – the head. In the past I've done it for my shoulder, but the head is more complicated. It took about 45 minutes and not only are you discouraged from moving even a *fraction* of an inch, but the operator also recommends you don't swallow. I challenge anyone to stop swallowing for 45 minutes, especially when you know you're not supposed to. It's torture!

That evening in an email link, I got the frightening images of my head's interior, along with the radiologist's notes. There was a bunch of blah, blah medical stuff, such as:

There is a vessel impinging on the inferior aspect of the right trigeminal nerve at its root (series 5000 image 76).

But the thing that stood out was:

The brainstem and cerebellum are unremarkable.

Unremarkable? How dare they! My cerebellum is fantastic! I think. Not sure exactly what it is and what it does, but I can assure you *and* the medical industry, that it is quite remarkable.

Five days later I went to my appointment. Dr. Rickins looked nothing like Franklin, but if I had to compare him to an American forefather, I'd say he was James Monroe with a beard. Dr. Rickens was also very nice. I suppose when you're dealing with people in pain, it helps to have good bedside manner. Of course, if you're being paid gobs of cash to do your job, that can bring out the sweetness in your personality as well.

Sitting on the examination table, Dr. Rickens gave me a brief overview of my issues and the solutions to the problem. There were three. I could…

1. continue to take medicine, which isn't completely effective, but helps
2. cut the nerve across my face, which is not only a temporary solution, but doesn't get to the root of the overall

problem, and could return in a few years; and finally…

3. get BRAIN SURGERY!

"What we do is cut a little door in the back of your skull," Dr. Rickens explained, "open it and move the nerve away from the artery that is throbbing against it, causing it to shock you."

Dr. Ricken says this as casually as one might describe any simple, everyday activity.

"We're just going to toss this moth we caught in the kitchen outside" or, "we're just going to slide this couch a foot to the right and center it below the painting."

I'm thinking: *is that right? Just open the skull and move the nerve? A little door you say? Do we install a doorknob? Perhaps a doorbell? Do we knock on the door? Hellllloooooo?* Bang, Bang, Bang. *Anyone in there?*

This is how doctors operate. Their work is so routine that brain surgery is a just another day in the office. My brother-in-law is the same way. He's an orthopedic surgeon and he's like: "We're just going to remove your leg and stick a metal leg back on… it's no big deal." Then the patient breaks down in tears. It's just another day on the job for him. These doctors do three-to-five of these operations a day. "Honey, I've scheduled five skull-openings on Monday and should be home for dinner. What are we having?"

Once the brain surgery info sunk deeper into my brain, I got woozy and almost passed out in Dr. Ricken's office. The doctor called his assistant, who rushed in to calm my nerves and lower the exam table so I could lie down. Apparently, I became ghost-white and clammy. It's not the first time that's happened to me in a medical setting. Debra offered me some candy, Jolly Ranchers, which are really good, and I particularly enjoy the watermelon flavor, but all I wanted was to fall asleep and pretend this never happened. After 20 minutes and a few sips of water, I was OK, and the doctor returned.

I told him I really needed to think things over. Everything's a little foggy after that. I left the office and did what I always do, and have so often done. I ignored everything for six months. I told everyone what the doctor said and vehemently stated that I will absolutely "NOT have brain surgery." I would continue the medication. Cutting the nerve on the face didn't appeal to me either. I was afraid of nerve damage to my face, which could cause drooping of the eye or mouth. So, I basically did nothing new.

That is, until the pain took over my life and I was debilitated. The pain emergency Dr. Patoni has warned me about had reared its ugly head – *my* ugly head.

I went through the five stages of surgery grief, except it was only three stages – and since I'd already gone through the *denial* part and the *bargaining* part, that left *acceptance* as the final domino to fall. My face and skull ached so badly I couldn't function. I could barely see. Four days of excruciating pain forced me to reconnect with Dr. Ricken. We had a video consultation and when I reminded him, *I was the weenie who almost passed out in his office*, he smiled and nodded... "I remember." The doctor confidently restated that it was time for the surgery. I agreed. Unfortunately, too much time had passed since I got my head MRI, so I needed to do it again. Then, we could meet for another face-to-face and go over the surgery and recovery plan.

The interior of the MRI room is like a nuclear bomb shelter. It's terrifying. You access through a massive metal door with warning stickers like "Beware of Radiation" and "Do Not Enter!" Except *you do* enter. It's a dark and windowless room, and there's warbling and hums akin to things that could easily blow up or fry you to a crisp. I feel more at ease in an earthquake.

The second MRI was an excruciating process. For some ungodly reason, I spent an hour and ten minutes inside the infernal tube. My first MRI was a swift 45 minutes. I'm not sure what happened during *this* MRI, but the longer it took, the more I began to doubt the woman manning the cacophonic contraption. I assumed the operator simply pushes a button on the MRI like one would do a microwave.

"Reheat"

"Popcorn"

"MRI"

"Here it is! MRI." *BEEP*!

But something went a bit haywire. Initially, she said it would be 20 minutes, then after an injection of contrast dye, an additional 20 minutes. At the one hour mark, while I was writhing in pain and beginning to unravel, her voice squeaked from the monitor.

"I want to run another section again. Can you do another ten minutes?"

Normally I have the patience of a two-year-old, and the thought of going through the MRI process *again* was both terrifying and exhausting, but I couldn't hack it anymore. 10 more minutes in the tube would have driven me certifiably insane, so I cried, "I can't do this anymore!" Somehow, she claimed it would only be five more minutes, and when I pushed back and said, "Is it really five minutes?" she replied after a pause, "I can do it in three and a half." It began to sound like a game show. I didn't realize it was negotiable. I also didn't know MRI machines were adjustable, but apparently, they are. Instead of "Defrost," she hit "Reheat." I remained corpse-like the entire three and a half minutes – the *envy* of the corpses in the building.

When released from the tomb of foam padding and ear plugs, I sat up and shook the stars from my vision like a cartoon crushed by a giant safe. She apologized, but I'm not sure anyone was to blame for this entire process. Maybe my mother. She told me she smoked and drank all through her pregnancy with me, and now it had come back to haunt me 53 years later in the form of choked facial nerves and brain stem dysfunction. Please ignore all previous writings about my own personal accountability with drug use, drinking, contact sports, falling, and general carelessness.

The following week. I met up with Dr. Ricken for a revised consultation. I spoke with his assistant on the phone, and we made a surgery date for August 18… end of summer. I wanted to enjoy the beach and get some sunshine before getting wrapped up like a mummy and tossed on the couch for three weeks.

During our first meeting, Dr. Ricken was bright and cheerful, but during the second consultation, he was tired and worn. It was a Friday, and I was tired too because most people are dragging their ass on Friday. Maybe he'd already done 30 or 40 of these surgeries and was tired of talking about heads, looking at brains, and dealing with people in general. Who knows? Maybe he was doing science experiments involving brain-swaps between patients and the results were disappointing. I'm not sure if there's a box to check on the hospital permission papers, but I will definitely check the DO NOT EXPERIMENT box on that form. I have my own issues. I don't want someone else's issues appearing in my mind.

Rita came with me during this consult, and he answered all 25 of my questions and all 25 of her questions. It was a lot of questions. If we had any more questions, we'd have to get another head because there's only so many questions you can ask as one patient.

•••

A few weeks later, I decided it was important to go to another neurosurgeon and get a second opinion on my surgery. That's what *they* say you should do. "Get a second opinion." That's what doctors say too, so I did that. I searched the internet and apparently there's only a handful of these specialists around. Then I had to research doctors that took my insurance. That narrowed the gauge again.

Then a friend of the family said he knew a doctor and recommended him highly because he hired him for a job in a hospital. An appointment was made, and I went to a late afternoon appointment a few days later.

Dr. Kerr was not only sweet, gentle and calm, but he whipped out a piece of paper and drew detailed diagrams of what was happening with my brain nerves. That information went in one ear and out the other, but the way he explained it at the time made perfect sense. An artery was rubbing the nerve and the channels in the nerve were rerouting… or something like that. He eventually compared it to a cable wire of some sort, and I started thinking about how shitty my cable service was, and perhaps it was bad because the wires were getting rubbed the wrong way.

Regardless, his argument for the surgery was convincing. I brought along a CD of my MRI, and he reviewed it on screen. The layered computer scans of my brain appeared in sections like thin-sliced ham, each slice showing various stages of the affected nerve. "You have a very typical type of Trigeminal Neuralgia" he said. That was good to hear because I didn't want a complicated form happening inside my brain. Dr. Kerr made me feel at ease.

But then, something happened during this consultation… I decided I wanted Dr. Kerr to perform my surgery. Not only were his online reviews perfect, but he was a friend to one of my parents' best friends. Not only that, but he would also perform the surgery at the hospital right around the corner from my house, one of the best hospitals in the state. I expressed to Dr. Kerr that I had trepidation about Dr. Rickens, and he understood, but confessed that he and Dr. Rickens were not only friends, but taught classes together, and I assumed he'd rat me out to Dr. Rickens and together they'd turn against me for being such an asshole about my surgeon.

"How dare he choose me and then choose you, Dr. Kerr!"

"Really! Who the hell does he think he is?"

I scheduled a surgery appointment with Dr. Kerr's assistant for August 19, and everything seemed ready to go.

Unfortunately, I had to call Dr. Ricken's office to tell them that I was a back-stabbing traitor and going with a different neurosurgeon. Denise was understanding and polite, assuring me I needed to, "do what was best for you." I got choked up at her sweet understanding. She was right, I needed to do what made me comfortable. But then I became uncomfortable because I began to doubt if I'd made the right decision.

"Was Dr. Rickens the better choice all along?"

"What if Dr. Kerr lobotomizes me?"

"What am I doing?"

These are all the questions one asks themselves when they're a stark, raving lunatic.

I have the same issue when I go to the grocery store. I'll take something off the shelf like a box white cheddar mac and cheese, then swap it with the box behind it on the shelf because the box I initially picked up was crushed or bent. Then, when I take the box home, I wonder if I should have taken the first box. Then I tragically realize that I took a box of *flaming hot* white cheddar mac and cheese and kick myself because I don't like spicy things like that. Was Dr. Kerr the flaming hot cheddar? Was Dr. Rickens the original flavor with only a minor bend in his packaging? These are the things that keep me up at night – more so than any stomach discomfort I get from flaming hot flavors.

Eventually, I found peace in my decision and enjoyed the flaming hot summer sun.

•••

For me, the idea of having brain surgery became acceptable. I was comfortable with it, even when my brain drifted to some dark places. Unfortunately, every time I mentioned the surgery to someone, even *doctors*, their reaction was like HOLY SHIT! YOU'RE GETTING A FUCKING HOLE DRILLED INTO YOUR HEAD? It didn't make life easy. It was unsettling. It would reset my expectations back to zero, which forced me to rebuild my confidence again.

The week leading up to the surgery was a mixture of emotions. Nervousness, no doubt, but a strange peace took hold, with an undertone of acceptance. The acceptance being the fact that I may die – although a very slight chance, still, a possibility. I tied up loose ends by making sure I scribbled on a piece of paper my last will and testament, which stated nothing more than: "I, A.J. Schmitz, being of sound mind (other than a painful nerve in the back of my skull), leave my house and car and all my belongings to my wife Rita and my son Max." Then I signed it and stuffed it in my briefcase which I assumed someone would look through when I died... at some point.

I also asked my sister to take care of Max and Rita should I die, and publish all my completed written works. But most of all, I prepared *myself* mentally for death. In my book *The Death of Our Dreams and Other Funny Stories*, I talk about the acceptance of death and how it made me live life in a fuller way. That still held true, but I needed to find true acceptance and peace again. Accepting death as a part of life is complicated, but once you do, you free yourself of fear, and begin to appreciate the little things life has to offer. But that feeling can wane the more addicted you get to life, especially if you have children you hope to raise into mature, functioning adults. You want to be around to help them make good decisions and cure them when they're ill. So, to booster the feeling of peace I had with death, I needed to accept that I could die on the operating room table, or even worse, never be the same physically and mentally again.

I even spoke to God, something out of the ordinary for me. On a long drive home from work one afternoon, I clipped the radio off and chatted with the big man, looking at the sky while gripping the steering wheel and occasionally pausing at traffic lights. That conversation is private, but the gist of it was being a better person, helping others, and doing more. Things desperate people with swelling hearts like to promise, usually around Christmas, or when they may die.

I then went to a pre-surgery check-in at Huntington Hospital where my surgery would be performed, and had an initial consultation where I signed papers with an incredibly polite woman named Stacy, who checked me in behind a wall of germ-bouncing glass. She was so calm and sweet, she felt like a warm cup of tea. She had little note cards where people could write a review and stuff it in a box, and I was planning on doing just that, writing the whole "cup of tea" thing I just stated, but she never asked and I forgot. I could picture the HR department reading my note and saying "awwww... isn't that sweet? Stacy is like a warm cup of tea. Glad she works for us!" Then I imagined they gave her a huge raise. Unfortunately, that scenario will never happen.

In the check-in examination room, a nurse asked me a million questions, most of them things she probably already knew because she had my sorted medical history at her finger-tips; but she interrogated me none-the-less. When she got to former recreational drug usage, I confessed to everything…

"Have you ever smoked cigarettes?"

"Yes."

"Have you ever used marijuana?"

"Yes."

"Have you ever used pain killers like Oxycodone?"

"Yes."

"Have you ever used Methamphetamines?"

"Yes."

"Have you ever used cocaine?"

"Yes."

"Have you ever used heroin?"

"Yes."

…I was responding to her questions like a robot, and it suddenly registered that I'd never used heroin and halted her before she hit SEND, or whatever she was entering into the database that would mark me for life in FBI files.

My favorite part of the exam was when the nurse had me point on a pain chart describing how much pain I could tolerate. It was a chart with an assortment of faces that start at 1, with a yellow smiley face, and descended to a 10, red crying face. I said I could tolerate the middle, 5 straight-mouth-in-a-line "green uncomfortable face," but in hindsight, I should have said 10, because if I'm uncomfortable in the hospital and press the nurse button, they'll look at my pain tolerance chart and say, "He's a 5, he can wait," when in reality, I'm a wussie and want nurses pampering me like a newborn baby. The visit concluded with a blood test where I nearly passed out, because I'm a huge wussie (as stated), and finally, a tutorial from the nurse about scrubbing my body with a special sponge to avoid bacteria. Considering the number of staph infections that have plagued hospitals over the years, I was willing to eat the sponge if necessary, but a few days of scrubbing in the shower would do just fine.

I solidified things at work, battened down the hatches of life, and went full speed ahead.

•••

I'm sure you've heard the horror stories before – true or not. A man goes into surgery for something simple like cataract removal or to reattach a rotator cuff and awakens to find both his legs missing below the knee… or even worse, both his testicles. Although extremely rare, these mix-ups occur. Of course, this is a paranoia I have because I'm an over-thinker who goes into every situation trying to predict and mentally prepare for every terrible scenario that may come from surgery. Things like heart attack on the table, waking up in the middle of the procedure, random earthquake while my skull is open, and of course – death.

To prevent this type of terrible mix-up in surgical procedures, hospitals cuff a wristband to you with a barcode, accompanied by your name and birth date, and then proceed to ask you to state, and *restate* your name and birth date, anywhere from 200 to 55,000 times so as not to be confused with the guy who needs both his legs amputated below the knees. This was evident from the jump when I went to my pre-surgery check in at the hospital a week before.

On Tuesday, the day of my surgery, my father drove Rita and I to the front entrance where we entered and checked in at the main desk. Up on the fourth floor, we came to a surgery check-in booth manned by a clean, smiling, and well-tanned man who bestowed upon me *that* wristband. He walked Rita and I to a desk around the corner where I checked into surgery and stated my name and birthdate for the second time. After I stripped naked and got into a gown, they placed me in a pre-surgery bed and jammed IV plugs into my arms and wrists.

By that point I'd reached a very calm mental state of mind. I was in the hands of the surgeons and nurses – all of them with the ability to kill or heal me, and I submitted completely. The main nurse asked me a barrage of questions about my past, including drug and alcohol use, which I admitted to freely, even though they have a complete history of my indiscretions already. After a long stretch of watching the "calm" channel on the TV above, where scenes of wildflowers blowing in the wind, eagles perched high on branches, and bubbling, babbling brooks lulled me into a stupor, the doctors paraded in.

So as not to become tedious, let me state now, that every single person, whether I was seeing them for the first or 50th time, asked me my name and birthdate, *and* asked me why I was there.

"Trigeminal nerve decompression surgery" was my answer, even though not exactly technically correct, was close enough to satisfy them.

Dr. Kerr, as pleasant a person as you'll likely meet, went over the procedure, how it was to be done, what was to be expected, and what the immediate aftermath would be like. He predicted a two-and-a-half-hour surgery, then took a purple marker and drew an R on the right side of my neck and circled it. I was a finally a Registered Trademark. Actually, that's to prevent him from amputating my testicles or other mix-ups like I spoke about, even though he's a neurosurgeon and shouldn't be anywhere near a set of testicles. After him, the main anesthesiologist Dr. Russo, his assistant Dr. Michaels, nurse aid one – Katie, who would be there to check for nerve interference control (or something like that - I'm not a doctor), and nurse assistant number two – Carla, who would be doing other stuff I'm not privy to, all asked me a variety of questions and I answered them as consistently as possible. They all asked if I was smoker or had smoked before. I said I quit smoking 20 years ago, but for some reason I still had a fear they'd cancel the surgery because I smoked Camel Lights by the carton in 1995.

The surgery team disappeared for a few hours (wildflowers, eagles etc.), until a nice doctor named Chen appeared (name/birthdate/etc.) and he wheeled me to the OR. I kissed Rita goodbye at a bank of elevators where she departed to the waiting area. It was like a movie. I watched my feet as they whirled around the hallways of the hospital, Dr. Chen's voice behind me as people passed by, said *hello*, said *excuse me*, or said something technical I didn't understand. I told Dr. Chen it was like a movie, and he agreed, "it does feel like that." He banged on a huge metal door and said, "Andrew Schmitz is here for surgery." My fear of being attacked by terrorists during surgery was alleviated because the main door was as big and thick as bank vault.

The OR was spacious. A massive metal room with equipment everywhere. If I saw a person monitoring the International Space Station, I wouldn't have been surprised. Nurse Katie was up high behind a monitor, looking down on the situation. There were giant TV screens against the walls – one set to a YouTube "Smooth Jazz" channel with the *play* button ready to be clicked. I felt like Robocop coming in to be reconstructed into the law enforcement machine of the future. Carla was waiting next to a thin surgery table where they slid me on like a fresh pizza. By the time I was on the table, I was in a state of total tranquility. Besides, I was in the same hospital where John Coltrane died, and if it was good enough for him, it was good enough for me.

I was assured I would go under anesthesia and awaken as if no time had passed at all. Carla asked me who I was, my birthdate, why I was there (missing legs, testicles, etc.), then she told me to imagine my favorite place.

I couldn't decide if it was a tropical beach or my sister's lake house, so I combined the two and BAM! I was out.

•••

Of the many things I was not prepared for during this process, was the way I'd feel after surgery. As I was awakened, I truly knew in that moment what the term, "death warmed over" felt like. It was, without doubt, the worst I've ever felt in any way, shape, or form in my entire life. Waiting in the recovery area with the anesthesia wearing off and awareness resurrecting me, the room spun wildly as vertigo took hold. I was nauseous, in writhing pain, and felt as if I was dying. My wife was there briefly to squeeze my hand, but I didn't want her to see me. I burst into tears.

Although the hospital was excellent in every way, the building itself couldn't hide its age. Going for a cat scan after the surgery, every uneven corridor section I entered that was stuck together over the years, and every elevator I was wheeled off across they're Grand Canyon-esque spacings, rattled my gurney like a jackhammer. I was reeling from discomfort, and the nurse apologized after each skull-rattling thump.

Finally recovering in the ICU, I received anywhere from 10 to 50 different drugs administered through either one of my three intravenous vein plugs, as well as orally. Every time a nurse came to dose me with some marble-mouthed concoction, I asked what it was for and was told it was either for pain, dizziness, potential infection, to help me shit, or to generally recover. I tried to remember the names for future documentation, but it was useless. Nurse Kate promised me she'd print them all out and leave it on my table before her shift ended, which she did. They consisted of names like: Dexamethasone, Hydromorphone, Cyclobenzaprine, Ondansetron, and Meclizine. Most of them more expensive than all my worldly possessions combined, I'm sure.

Besides the pain of having a hole in my skull "the size of a quarter" and sealed with a metal plate, was the fact I had 20 metal staples clamping my wound (the size of a half dollar) shut, which made it impossible to find head comfort regardless of which way I flipped and flopped. My only comfort was a constant routine of two pain killers, which lasted no more than two hours and could only be administered every four to six hours. It was a cruel leapfrog scenario that forced me to bide my time until relief came, or predict when the pain would come, which I never did until I was in pain. Matt, my first nurse, was required to wake me every hour for a "neuro check" where I raised my hands, lifted my legs, occasionally squeezed his hands, stated my name, birthdate and location, and was made delirious from lack of sleep and stabbing pain.

Although I did have a new and exciting hole in my head, not much discomfort compared to having my catheter removed. More shocking was the fact that I didn't know I had a catheter in! If you don't know what a catheter is, it's a long tube that goes up your urethra to drain your urine. When Matt slipped in and announced he was going to remove my catheter, I was like "whaaaaa?" Those drugs were working better than I realized. He said it would be a little *uncomfortable*, and I asked him to give it to me straight…

"It's really uncomfortable, isn't it?" He admitted, "yeah, it's pretty uncomfortable." That's the kind of nurse I like. No bullshit.

Well, he wasn't kidding. I nearly hit the roof. When he slid that sucker out of my penis, it felt like he was conducting a jagged New York City subway through. Holy shit. It was literally a hair-raising experience. I believe getting reamed by a rhino is less uncomfortable.

On day two, while Hurricane Erin was creeping up the coast towards Long Island, nurse Melanie blasted into my room. A force of nature I was not prepared for, Melanie may have been my saving grace. Of course, all nurses are to be commended for the wonderful work they do, but Melanie may have endured my worst. She was older, perhaps 60, and a wily vet. Her instincts outweighed her bedside manner. At one point she was shouting from my room to another nurse for help, even though she was tying my gown and her mouth was about six inches from my ear. Her motherly instincts may have been more useful than her nurse's education. She predicted my every need, made sure I was completely comforted before she left the room (mainly so I didn't ring the infernal nurse bell), and stood strong as I vomited most of the day.

At midday, a Physical Therapist came and forced me to take a walk. Taking advantage of standing, Melanie thought it was prime time for me to pee, which I hadn't done without a catheter yet. Standing half naked and flanked by two women, Melanie holding the plastic urinal and the Physical Therapist holding my gown open, I tried to get comfortable and release. In my groggy state, I was finding it hard to *handle* myself, so Melanie grabbed my penis and essentially tossed it into the urinal's opening like one might toss a hose into a flowerpot. She then made pee noises, which didn't have the desired effect she thought. I was tempted to ask, "you ladies come here often?" but wasn't sure how it would fly after reading the room. After a minute, I managed to pee while thinking it was perhaps one of the most awkward situations I'd likely find myself in ever again.

Although Melanie was enthusiastic about my urination, trumpeting my skills like that of a child going in the toilet after years in a diaper, the Physical Therapist was less enthusiastic about my walking skills. She felt I was shuffling, and not stepping confidently like a person would normally walk. I agreed, as I was loaded with drugs, and donning a fresh hole in my head. I felt like an 80-year-old man, and was determined to never feel like that again, even when I am an

80-year-old man. I then sat in a recliner chair and zonked out for a few hours.

Later Dr. Kerr came with two other doctors – all of them happy with the results, my appearance, and the early recovery. Dr. Kerr whipped out his cell and flipped through a series of photos of my opened skull, showing in graphic, stomach-churning detail the nerves, arteries and other gory things in my skull. I looked at the photos confidently and with fascinated attention, but if I wasn't completely whacked on drugs, I would have passed out from the sight. I almost puked, but I was already vomiting throughout the day, so I couldn't say the photos produced that result.

Later, I wondered who took the photos of my head... Dr. Kerr or someone else because cell phones are a Petrie dish of infectious germs and whipping a cell phone from your pocket mid-surgery seems like a no-no. Maybe it was steril-ized, I don't know, or perhaps a nurse came in and snapped them, but with the number of precautions they took before the surgery, I assume they took the necessary steps. Later that evening I ate some chicken soup and plain rice and kept it down without hurling.

My family came to say hello during a peak high on pain meds – greeting them with a stupid grin and lidded eyes. They gave me cards and well wishes. My son drew Wolverine on his card, which was very well done. Then, during an ex-tended talk about medical procedures, my son nearly fainted and had to sit in my lounger, rescued by the steadfast Melanie, who sparked him back to life with jokes and ginger ale. Like father, like son.

Early the next morning, Dr. Kerr arrived with two other doctors and remove the bandage that was wrapped around my head. I didn't realize how much pressure the bandage was applying, because after its removal, I felt an amazing sense of release as the blood rushed to my hair. The gauze patch over the wound remained though, and Dr. Kerr snuck a look, satisfied with the healing process.

After Melanie, came nurse Matt again, and the next day I was moved to a "step-down" unit a few rooms down the hall – meaning, I was good enough to come off 24-hour observation.

My first nurse on the step-down unit was Ally. A pale brunette, she was soft-spoken, but all business. I took a walk with her around the ward, and it was clear early in the conversation that my pain medicine intake would be severely reduced. Because of the international opioid epidemic, the medical industry distributed drugs very cautiously. You must *completely* sell your pain to the nurses like an actor going for a golden statuette during Oscar season. Even though I had a newly burrowed hole in the head, the side glances were evident.

"Yes, the hole in my skull and the 20 razor-sharp staples clawing me like forks are a slight discomfort. May I please have some pain meds?"

My *last* ICU room, 164, was dreadfully boring. I sat in either the bed or the lounge chair and literally faced the blank wall for two days, which was preferable to anything because of vertigo. In my new room, S58, I faced a TV with a whopping 14 channels, most of them pre-set to either bland news, Spanish soap operas, or other channels no one with cable or internet access watches. Fortunately, they had ESPN, where for the next 24 hours I watched the talking heads yell at each other about the Dallas Cowboys trading their star player and nothing else. It was a slow August news cycle. I took in a few low-ranking US Open tennis matches, but they were only slightly more stimulating than the blank wall.

Ally was relieved of duty by the bright, perky blonde Katie, who had multiple assistants, most prominently an older Asian woman named Chloe. Like Melanie, Chloe was a vet who buttoned everything up tight, and insisted she stand behind me while I urinated in my private bathroom. The last time I urinated in front of so many strangers was in the men's room at a Knicks game. Still, it was better than constantly using the confounding plastic urinal container in my bed, whose strange angle and cursed handle forced me on more than one occasion to accidentally geyser on the bed and myself. Combined with not bathing or brushing my teeth for three days, I began to smell like the men's room at a Knicks game.

Dr. Kerr made his final appearance to remove the gauze from my wound, husking diligently, perplexed by the amount of tape used to seal it tight. Once removed, he took his trusty cell phone, snapped a picture and flashed his handy work. Like a Frankenstein movie, the grisly stitch job wasn't unlike the ghastly chop job strewn across the noggin' of the neck-bolted monster. Again, the removal of the gauze patch was a relief, pointing me towards normalcy. Dr. Kerr was easily the correct choice for this delicate job and his enthusiasm for his skilled work was matched only by me, knowing I was in good hands.

•••

Friday, under the care of nurse Orelia, I signed some papers, was asked about my home care from a social worker, then was released back into the wild – my family waiting outside for me in the bright sunshine. My father drove me home, and I gingerly took a spot on the couch where I battled dizziness, vertigo, pain, discomfort and lack of sleep for the next 10 days. Slowly improving, I graduated from the small steps of shuffling around the house, to giant leaps of shuffling up and down the driveway. My wife scolded me for my "old man" shuffle, but a week later, I was circumnavigating the neighborhood with confident steps. Although my mind was as sharp as a steel trap, my head felt like it was *caught* in a steel trap from the staples clamped into my head causing me endless agony, making it impossible to find a comfy spot no matter how many times I flipped my body or twisted my pillow into various cloth croissants.

Before I was released from the hospital, Dr. Kerr insisted that I drink a lot of water, and I did, by the pool-load – but with the parade of pills I gobbled through the process, I became so constipated I didn't shit for 10 days. I took a prescription laxative that worked, but then my body did a 180 and instilled a volcanic bout of diarrhea that nearly caused me to pass out. Having purified myself completely, I was lighter, returning to some semblance of regularity, in more ways than one. My final hurdle was our bird Zen, who mercilessly tweeted (more like shrieked) around the clock, which echoed through my sensitive skull like a police whistle.

Through the process was nurse Rita, my benevolent wife, who having been personally squeezed through the anxiety wringer before, during, and after the surgery, cared for me until she nearly dropped from exhaustion. The sense of worry from my family, especially my wife and son, who looked stressed and pale (regardless of summer tans), and my parents and sister, whose jaws were wound tighter than piano wire, was palpable. When the color returned to my cheeks, the hair grew back on my shaved head, and the fall schedules fell into place, the world was right again and a sigh of relief fell over us all.

Back in front of the esteemed Dr. Kerr and his staff, I finally had the irritating staples removed. Nurse Jessica carefully plucked them off, each one hurting the tender skin more than the other. My wife documented each stage of the healing process through photos, although each one appeared the same to me. Once the staples were removed, the gruesome gash was more apparent, and the staple holes that remained resembled the Frankenstein monster's skull more than before. The crusty, coagulating cut with 'suture' holes pocking along its route felt slightly antique. Surely there was a better way to bore into a skull with more grace than was shown, but apparently not. I mean, what were they to do? Go in through the mouth? The eyeball? The asshole? I suppose this was the way it worked and that was what I had to live with.

I didn't realize my vanity would come to fruition so strongly. Having visited the supermarket over the years wearing nothing but rags and hair bent at angles like a man caught in high winds, I tended to care less. But cut a hole in my head and suddenly I felt exposed. Like I'd been marked by a hideous scarlet letter that people noticed a parking lot away. I wore hats to the supermarket to hide my head. Not only did I not want people looking at me, I didn't have the energy to engage in conversations about my procedure. I was still dizzy and off-balance – the buzzing blue glare and labyrinth-like shelving of the supermarket stunting me ill to begin with. But to yap with an old lady in the condiment aisle about my surgery would easily make me puke, and vomiting in the market is a blow to anyone's vanity regardless of your skull's condition.

The staple removal did little for my comfort. I thought it would be an instant relief, and it *was* on the surface, but the sting of the staples were masking the underlying pain of the hole in my skull, which was swollen and throbbing. The skin on the right side of my head was pulled tight, along with the skin on my neck, both yanked taught to meet in the middle at the skull base where they were clamped together for the rest of their days. Dr. Kerr encouraged me to twist my head in a series of exercise to keep loose, which I did, but the process would take a while. The nerves under my hair tingled, making new pains similar to being hit in the head with a dense, hard object.

The days got better and better, yet sleep eluded me. I had one comfortable position to lay on, my left ear, and after three weeks, that poor ear became irritated and raw. Almost becoming the cauliflower ear of a wrestler. I had one red, scaling left ear, and one slightly deaf, protruding right ear. Vanity, at that point, was long gone. I spent many days recovering outside under an umbrella on our new outdoor furniture, and read cards from family and friends, while fielding text messages of love from cousins and buddies, some of whom I hadn't heard from in quite some time.

My wife chauffeured me around because I wasn't allowed drive a car for six to eight weeks. Being a bit of a control freak, I didn't love it, but after a while I didn't mind so much. Unfortunately, I became one of those annoying backseat drivers (even though I was in the front seat) pointing constantly about choice parking spaces, people mindlessly crossing the road, and traffic lights destined to turn red.

Also, by doctors' orders, I was not allowed to lift heavy things, an order I enjoyed immensely. Anything from yanking the garbage out of the can and hauling it to the curb, to scooping firm ice cream, needed to be done by either my wife or my son, and after a while it became borderline hedonistic for me. I would command something be done under the guise of feebleness from surgery, and my command was executed. After a while I tried to bleed that power beyond its rational purpose and was met with steely glares, especially when it came to things like making them dip potato chips into sour cream and hauling it my mouth on the couch.

Many recovery issues I faced along the way like headaches and general pain was expected. I knew there'd be a few I didn't expect. But one I didn't see coming, literally, was my eyesight getting worse. Like, a lot worse! My glasses didn't seem to work anymore, and I squinted at everything even though I wore them. What did improve, for some strange reason, was my sense of smell. I don't know how the brain works, but my sense of smell was so strong, I could taste and smell things I'd never smelled before. Some odors made me nauseous. I'm not sure swapping eyesight for smell was a good tradeoff, but I assumed it was all temporary.

Another unforeseen issue was the arm of my eyeglasses creating a large dent on the side of my head as it swelled. I began wearing the arm over my right ear, which eventually got as raw and red as the left ear that was pressed against the pillow each night. Soon, there was no comfort to lay down, and the idea of sleeping standing like horse was almost preferable.

Three weeks after my surgery, after some tolerable sleep, some long walks, and a multitude of good meals, I worked from home (so I didn't go bankrupt) until I returned to my office in late October.

•••

Three months after surgery, I began to slowly come off the nerve-blocker Oxcarbazepine. Dr. Kerr felt it was time to ween off and see the effectiveness of the surgery. Along with Nurse Jessica, we agreed to halve the two doses until it was zero, because to come off too abruptly could cause a seizure, a tidbit of info that nearly threw me into another bout of swirling panic and dizziness.

Less than two months after that, I was completely off the medicine.

Over two years on nerve-blockers caused my body to acclimate, and coming off made me feel everything from foggy, distant, and apathetic, to borderline crazy, which was another in a long line of things I was not prepared for. I suppose if I'd had a list of all the complications, side effects, and potential problems I may have faced along the way, as well as other answers to my many, many questions, I may not have

had the surgery at all. Keeping patients with overactive imag-
inations and a proclivity to pass out at the mere mention of
the words, blood, needle or cut "in the loop" is nothing but a
losing game.

Six Months after surgery, at the end of February, I felt
about 90 percent. One of my concerns about the surgery was
never really being the same physically. That concern proved
to be true; but who was I kidding? I was 54 and not going to
wrestle the title of World's Strongest Man from the guy who
last won the World's Strongest Man Competition. That's the
competition where those massive dudes lift boulders up on
pedestals and yank locomotives around with rope. How those
guys don't blast a hernia out of their asshole, I'll never know.
But I was back at the gym, running (not a four-minute-mile),
and doing light weights and doing it without pain. Life was
OK.

My ragged ears returned to normal, my smell restored
to its factory setting of terrible, and my eyesight sharpened,
although back to its post-factory setting of bad.

Hopefully this is the final stage of my head issues.
But I doubt it. I was told Trigeminal Neuralgia can return in
about 10 years, on average, and if it did return for me, I could
"just get the surgery again!"

I'm not sure having brain surgery at 64 is the way to
go, but I'm not sure being randomly electrocuted in the face at
64 is the way to go either. Perhaps I could take the Oxcarbazepine again. And of course, there's a third option.

I can ignore it.

Because as history has shown, that's *always* an effective cure to health issues.

Lunch Guy

For years our marketing group worked in a big office building in Melville, New York. It was a standard, multi-box complex – devoid of charm and mostly a cold, dystopian cement block in the middle of a parking lot with enough parking spots to accommodate three Super Bowls simultaneously. Another building among the thousands you've passed a thousand times down some stretch of road at 60 miles per hour, even though the speed limit is 40. I'd occasionally get lost in that building because each bank of elevators was completely indistinguishable from another. Just a wash of beige and grey with the occasional potted plant to give the place a hint of life and to separate "areas."

But the one saving grace of the building was the restaurant in the basement. I use the term restaurant loosely. It was more like a high-end school cafeteria. Owned and run by a Mexican woman named Sheila, they made solid sandwiches and often had a taco bar, which was excellent, as you might imagine from a Mexican owner. The people who worked there were nice and the prices reasonable. They offered cozy booths, solid wooden tables, and the place exuded a heaping dose of charm – the charm coming from the fact that it was formerly some sort of 1980s Irish pub/pizza place, with green walls, dense wood molding, and rows of low-hanging, green glass lights that sparkled with golden hues against the brass holdings.

Then one day, my boss found us a new office building. It was an immediate upgrade. Besides being 15 minutes closer to my home, the modern office space we occupied was a prestigious corner spot, giving us big windows that flooded the place with light and a decent view. That view was the back of a Staples office supply store, but there were trees, and it was better than my previous view of a lifeless gray wall. The rent was also cheaper, which of course, my boss loved.

Unfortunately, there were negatives. Aren't there always? At the top of the list of the building's many issues, was the overall design. The architects must have either been on acid, or lunatics inspired by Frank Gehry, where form almost always trumps function. Unfortunately, Frank Gehry was a genius, and these hack architects were *most certainly* not. In fact, I don't think they were architects at all, but a band of rouge lawyers asked to piece together something both dangerous and hard to escape. This place was the opposite of the simple, lifeless block we previously inhabited. It was an over-engineered mess.

Originally a high school constructed in the mid 1950s, its layout consisted of random sections puzzled together through confounding staircases, half floor landings, miles of wasted space, and random hallways that led to nowhere. Besides coffee, my daily routine consisted of me asking, "who the hell made this design choice?" There was a 'West' building and an 'East' building, but considering the construction had no more thought to it than a UPS guy stacking boxes in the back of a truck, it seemed pointless. I'm sure every 1950s high school student received tardy marks having spent the first month of their schooling figuring out the perplexing amalgamation of spaces, landings and squares.

Although I usually entered through a side door, whenever I came in through the main lobby, I'd invariably find a despondent elderly person scratching their head in front of the ridiculously confusing guide board. Each office space was given a mystifying series of numerical and linguistic suffixes that even *we*, the tenants of the building, couldn't understand. 201WB was literally next to 303EF. Later, we'd come to find the building had also delineated a 'Front' and 'Back' even though when you faced the building from the street, the building's entrance was on the side. We could never understand where the front of the building was in comparison to the back. Not only that, but the West portion of the building also actually faced East. When someone needed help finding an office they were scheduled to visit, I'd take a trip with them and discover new and exciting sections never before visited. Many of our clients found themselves lost in the corn-maze of the building, calling us in desperation from their cells to be rescued, and brought safely to our office.

Another negative of the building was the lack of basement restaurant to grab an easy lunch… or so I thought. After a month in our new digs, I was informed by my workmate

Ross that there was indeed a place to eat in the basement. A deli. I didn't even know the building *had* a basement, but I also didn't know it had a gym and a pharmacy, two things I discovered while wandering the grounds, having accidentally exited an emergency door somewhere in the West/Back building.

Despite the fact that I have a decent sense of direction, after two failed attempts to find the basement deli, I resigned to the fact I needed Ross's help to locate the place, a journey that apparently consisted of visiting another embankment of lobbies (Back or West), a painfully slow elevator ride down, then about 15 left turns which you'd think would make you go around in endless circles, but apparently not.

As Ross and I ventured out to find the deli, I didn't need Ross's help because Jorge the building manager, discovering I was going to the deli, decided to show me a 'secret' way to get there. Bypassing the entrance to the main lobby, Jorge and I circled down another half landing of stairs to what seemed to be the lower floor (but not a basement) where we took a sharp turn through a non-descript door, down a slim set of brightly lit stairs, and through a labyrinth of underground halls so complicated, it took me the better part of the third quarter to remember the ridiculous pattern. I thought for sure Jorge was leading me to my untimely death as we passed multiple doors with non-descript banging and grinding, as well as little snippets of creepy music wafting from hand-held radios. Eventually we turned a corner and there it was – the deli.

I use the term deli loosely.

Owned and run by Glen, a man older than dirt, the place was wedged into a forgotten side alcove lost in time.

Glen was quiet, grim, and very rarely spoke. He reminded me of Kevin McCallister's neighbor in the movie *Home Alone* – old man Marley, who everyone thought was a serial killer. Glen didn't give off those kinds of vibes, but he wasn't exactly a charming ball of bubbly either. He'd take your order and slowly turn to make it, rotating like an obsolete robot on its last detail.

Like the Mexican restaurant in our last building, the deli felt like a relic leftover from a different organization. The Mexican place was great, but it was housed in an old Irish pub, which made you question why anyone felt the need to build an Irish pub in the basement of a beige industrial complex in the first place, next to the janitor's station and humming furnaces. The pub had its awkwardness, but its green lights and fabric patterns resembling train seat coverings from 1979 had square peg charm that fit neatly into the building's round hole. Glen's deli was just a grubby, dirty hole, that didn't fit anywhere. The browning alcove was equipped with foggy glass cases filled with chopped salads in mismatched Corningware dishes, faux wooden countertops curling at the edges, and rusting slicers and grill presses that somehow survived the bombings of Pearl Harbor. Every square inch of wall space surrounding Glen's deli was painted neon-white – all of it presented under oppressive fluorescent lights, giving everything an unsettling tinge of electric blue, yet highlighting the deli alcove's yellowing decay even more. Much like the little house that refused to give up its plot for the city planners, it eventually had a series of skyscrapers built up around it.

Also bordering on ancient was Glen's drink coolers and storage units. The open-faced cooler, which in most establishments can be seen wafting with cold, dense air, was just Glen's shelving unit for random items. One warm summer day I reached for what I believed to be an ice-cold Milky Way bar, only to be met with a luke-warm chocolate bar, limping under the system's intense lights. Ross and I would come in for cold drinks and find the refrigerator broken and the ice cream floor unit stuffed to the sliding glass top with soda bottles.

Also lost in time were Glen's prices. I came to the deli from an overlong morning meeting and was starving for breakfast. I ordered a bagel with cream cheese and was asked for a dollar in return. Lunch, no matter what kind of sandwich you ordered and piled with ingredients, came to a mere $5. I didn't complain, but I couldn't understand how Glen made any money. Candy bars were fifty cents, and a coke was a buck. You couldn't leave most delis at that time without forking over a $20 bill, yet somehow you could eat at Glen's Lost-In-Time lunch cavern with the rattling change you scraped together from your car's drink holder.

Also, among the many curiosities, was knowing whom Glen was actually affiliated with. Although all the food seemed fresh and safe, there didn't seem to be any board of health codes posted on the wall. There were no inspection notices, no health grades, and not even the standard 'what to do in a choking emergency' poster. Not only was there no credit card option, Glen never rang anyone up on a register or produced a receipt for a bill of sale. No tax was added to the price, everything came out evenly, and money was handled over the counter with change given directly from his pocket.

Up on a beat up, dusty wooden shelf in the corner of the ceiling was a small television set, where Glen played the TV show *Seinfeld* on a constant rotation. He owned the complete collection on DVD where I could dependably catch 10 minutes of classic moments. That ran for almost two years when suddenly, *Seinfeld* was cast aside for live Phish concerts, which seemed like a strange choice for a guy who may have been raised on Duke Ellington. Although he was most likely raised on Rock 'N Roll, the basement's poor airflow system and feeble lighting sucked two decades from his complexion. Stranger still, was the level at which he set the volume… obnoxiously loud. Going through my secret back way through the crime scene hallway towards the deli, I could hear the distinctive guitar noodling of Trey Anistacio at wall-trembling volumes. This wasn't a man enjoying music… this was a statement.

In an opposite alcove across from the deli were four hard, Formica picnic table booths, used only by Ross in the two years I worked there. And Ross would wear headphones so he could block out *Seinfeld* and watch movies on his computer. But once Phish came on the scene, the Formica tables disappeared, and Glen's grim attitude became decidedly morose.

While plopping a dollop of tuna salad on wheat toast with a rusty ice cream scooper, I finally broke down and gave Glen the once-over… dug into who the man was and what his life may have been like. Through a series of quiet grunts and mini-statements, Glen confessed that new management (the son of the building owner *of course*), was determined to kick Glen out of there and build a proper lunch station. Why they couldn't do that with an experienced deli man like Glen at the forefront, I couldn't say, but his days were definitely numbered.

At our old building, the Mexican lunch spot was packed with people daily. Hundreds of people shuffled in and out in a constant food rotation. At Glen's deli, the only person I ever saw besides Ross, was a dark-haired kid no more than 20, who ordered a bagel. Then I never saw him or anyone else again in the two years I visited.

Days after our stimulation conversation, Glen was gone. I turned the corner one day to find the entire crusty deli empty, save for some dust bunnies, a stray electrical cord, and few flattened candy wrappers that'd been trapped under heavy equipment for years. Even though I'd barely spoken five words to the man before our in-depth conversation, I felt bad for him. I believe the deli was his life. It was probably his only income, even though he was practically giving food away. Perhaps Glen had spent so much time underground, he didn't realize the world changed and food prices had risen considerably. But once he was gone, it felt like a small heartbeat in the chest of the building disappeared.

Not long after his departure, the management began mounting large, fancy Lucite signage on the walls, fastened with modern silver disc studs. On the signs, besides completely irrelevant arrows pointing to the East, West, Front and Back sections of the complex, was the noticeable verbiage of *cafeteria*. How anyone would get there without two Sherpa and a satellite map, I wasn't sure, but the Lucite signs were accompanied by flyers encouraging us to raise our excitement to crack-cocaine levels for the forthcoming new cafeteria.

As the winter came and everyone's desire to go outside for lunch dwindled, the announcement that the cafeteria was officially open for business (via more flyers) was met with a small amount of curiosity. Very few things raise the blood pressure of the average office worker more than knowing a new food source has entered your world. It's something to celebrate, no matter how inconsequential it is in the grand scheme of things.

A few days later, Ross and I decided we'd take a lunchtime stroll to our new cafeteria and have a bite to eat. Maybe the Formica booths had returned where we could sit and reminisce about Glen and the old deli. Or maybe recall some of the funnier *Seinfeld* moments that tickled our funny bones… specifically, bits that took place in the booth at Monk's Café, the diner they frequented on the show.

When Ross and I rounded the corner, we were not met with gleaming glass cases of egg salad, or old deli men ready to serve us in crisp white linen aprons. We were met by two HUGE, towering, futuristic vending machines that looked as if they'd been programmed to eliminate humanity in a film about cyborg hitmen. If Glen was a small heartbeat in the industrial complex, then these machines were certainly the artificial heart meant to replace him. To add insult to injury, the two vending machines were the only two things in this newfangled "cafeteria." There were no benches, no chairs, no services and certainly no audience laughter as Kramer stumbled into Jerry's apartment after a series of social observations went sideways.

To make matters worse, even though the vending machines were brand new, and were something the Japanese lived with daily and used as frequently as we here in America used a faucet, they already appeared to be malfunctioning. Someone posted an angry note (flyer) to the window of the sandwich machine, stating defiantly that the machine had eaten her money for lunch, and rudely not dispensed a lunch for her to eat in return. Ross and I didn't want to risk our hard-earned cash, so we split.

I visited the vending machines a few more times to see if things were running smoother, but each time I visited, the contents of triangle-cut tuna sandwiches and cheese & nut packets seemed to slowly dissipate until there was nothing in the machines at all. My last visit came after both machines were removed, and nothing but a stark white room remained where the overly waxed linoleum flooring caught the light of the obnoxious fluorescent light rods above.

I often wondered what happened to Glen and where he may be working, if he was working at all. It didn't seem like his little hole in the ground was a major nuisance, but management felt differently. They ousted him and then fumbled the reinvention. It all seemed like a colossal waste. Another empty alcove in a building filled with them.

Because the "cafeteria" was a complete failure, I was forced to venture out, which was serendipitous because I discovered one of the best sushi places in town hiding in plain sight. A dark little hole no bigger than Glen's deli, but presided over by a master sushi chef who loaded up the plates with tasty Japanese fare.

Unfortunately, at today's prices.

World's Dumbest Smart Person

I'm the world's dumbest smart person.

Or the world's smartest dumb person. Take your pick.

All through my school years, I learned and retained everything there was to know about the things I loved… movies, comic books, music, pop culture, and sports. I was an awful student who barely passed my classes. Then, when I was older, I learned all the things I should have learned when I was in school… history, art history, science, and sociology – all the things that would have made me a better student. Except for math. I use math sporadically and when I do use it, it's on my phone calculator.

I tend to approach things backwards. I'll assemble a piece of furniture, then look at the instructions and note how much easier it would have been to read them before I started killing myself with the project. I'm a visual learner, so reading things doesn't always help me. But the self-assembly furniture directions are usually pictograms, so they're universal to all languages, with lots of screws going into holes, and arrows pointing at objects – featuring those faceless, round-headed people you see on bathroom signs, so I don't know why I don't use the instructions. Maybe I'm stubborn. It's not a smart way to approach things.

I'm smart, but not *smart* smart.

When I watch *Jeopardy!* I get something in range of 5 to 20 questions correct. Memory retention is not exactly intelligence. The ability to problem-solve is more of a sign of intelligence, but that's just my theory. I'm not a psychologist. Problem solving intelligence is called *Logical-Mathematical* Intelligence. I have a high IQ, but that's because I have *Visual Intelligence*.

There are 8 types of intelligence. Musical, Visual-Spatial, Linguistic, Logical-Mathematical, Bodily-Kinesthetic, Interpersonal, Intrapersonal, and Naturalistic. If you have none of these, you're stupid… or perhaps worthless. I assume most intelligent people have multiple types of intelligence, but making that kind of assumption isn't very smart.

I'm a writer with a decent vocabulary, but I'm not a *Lexicomane* or a *Sesquipedalian*. Trust me, I had to look up the word Sesquipedalian online. A Lexicomane is someone with a deep vocabulary (more specifically, combs through dictionaries) and a Sesquipedalian means someone who overuses long words. It may not even be a real word. I found it on the internet, so there's a 60% chance it's not factually correct. Where did I get the number 60% from? I made it up. If I post it online, it may become fact. My vocabulary isn't large enough to contain the word Sesquipedalian anyway. There isn't exactly a specific word for someone with a large vocabulary, per se. That seems odd because you'd think a large vocabulary would have its own word. A word that no one uses except those with large vocabularies.

David Foster Wallace was a writer with an extensive vocabulary. That's probably why his book *Infinite Jest* is over 1,000 pages. He couldn't shut up. I love long books with challenging words, but I don't want to read it for six months because I spent half the time referencing a dictionary. I read *Mark Twain* by Ron Chernow, which was over 1,000 pages, and I enjoyed it, but the number of words I didn't understand was considerable. I looked some of them up, but after a while I just tried to figure out what the word meant based on the context of the situation and the words that came before it in the sentence. That's *Linguistic Intelligence.*

I have what is called general vocabulary anxiety, which for the most part is a fear of using words incorrectly… or, fear of embarrassing myself with Malapropism usage. That's the unintentional misuse of a word that sounds like the correct word you should have used. I like the sounds of words and will toss them in because I believe they fit, but later find the context is completely wrong, which makes me sound like an ignoramus. I know the word ignoramus because my grandfather used to say that a lot. Not to me, but in general because I believe it was a word one level higher than idiot, and ignoramus rolls off the tongue nicely.

My intelligence is structured around my small world and the context that lies therein. I know a lot about movie history, but there's always someone who knows more. I'm more of a dabbler… a skimmer of movie history. I can hold a conversation with the biggest movie buffs and historians, but I can't dive so deep I'm reference supporting actors from 1920s German films. Same with Jazz music. I studied Jazz history and have listened to a lot of Jazz music, but I don't know everything. Not by a long shot. I know a little bit about a lot of things. That's what some people call "a jack of all trades and a master of none." That's good for cocktail parties when different groups mix, but not when you're taking tests, or when you're on a gameshow where thousands of dollars are on the line. Like *Jeopardy!* If I went to a Jazz conference, I'd be lost, but if someone asks me what my favorite Charles Mingus album is, I have the answer, followed up by knowledge of his other works.

I play chess, a game that's associated with high intelligence, but I'm not very good. I'm okay. I rarely win. If I play someone good, I'll occasionally illicit a "nice move" from them, or perhaps a "didn't see that coming," followed by a smirk, but it rarely ends with me check-mating my opponent. I can kick a lot of people's asses in checkers, which is like chess for dummies, but then a precocious eight-year-old will come along and wreck me by triple-jumping me, getting a King, then bounding back to their side of the board while taking the rest of my pieces.

There are folks who think people with large vocabularies have an air of superiority about them. These intellectuals invoke images of men wearing monocles and women donning long white gloves – all of them sipping champagne. Perhaps those Sesquipedalians are over-educated, or, simply hold advanced degrees in the fields of literature or language. I don't judge them, but I would like to know what the hell they're talking about. I'm not sure why you'd want to have such a massive vocabulary. Most people… you know, the downtrodden and sad, won't know what you're saying and perhaps that's the point. These high-vocabulary people prefer to stay in their own esteemed group, excluding the dregs of society.

My friend John once said he felt the word *Oxymoron* was an unnecessarily complicated word when the word *Contrary* would do. He has a point, but I like the word oxymoron because it contains the word *Moron*. I'm not sure what that has to do with anything, but when oxymoron is used correctly, it makes you feel as though a strong and valid argument has been made. Like when you point out the use of words in media when terms like *Radical Conservative* are tossed around.

"The radical conservative blew up the abortion clinic because of his beliefs."

I think once you blow something up with explosives, the word conservative is excised from your title. Personally, I think the word *Verisimilitude* is a far more long and complicated word than necessary when the word *realistic* or *plausibility* would do. I feel that way because I've been trying to find a way to use verisimilitude in a conversation for decades and have yet to find the opportunity. When the time comes, I'll probably say it incorrectly because of that vocabulary malapropism anxiety thing, and embarrass myself in front of a group of intellectuals who will guffaw in my face, and banish me from the conversation to go mingle with the wait staff serving the champagne. By the way, the fear of long words is called *Hippopotomonstrosesquipedaliophobia*, which is an oxymoron if I ever saw one.

If you want to test your ability to properly characterize the definition of a word, have children. They'll inevitable ask what a word means and it's your job to tell them the literal dictionary definition of the term.

"Dad, what does *because* mean?"

You brain whirls to a halt like the thickened contents of a blender.

"Because? It means… because! OK?! It means because!"

Then you begin to think about the dictionary definition of *all* words; words you thought did the defining for you. It's a rabbit hole you can't escape, and the more you think about these words, the more you realize you don't know anything, really.

When people aren't book smart, they're called "street smart." That's a polite way of saying they're dumb, but in reality, they understand their surroundings (Interpersonal Intelligence) and won't get mugged because their nose is buried in a book or lost in their thoughts (Intrapersonal Intelligence). In the southern states of America, they say "bless your heart," which a polite way of saying, "you're an idiot," but it almost comes across as compliment. Intelligent people toss out, "you're ill-informed," which seems like a firm way of saying, "You don't know the subject well enough to comment," but in reality, it's similar to saying, "you're dim." Stupid people are too dumb to be shy, so they just say, "You're a dumb-ass!" If a stupid person is calling you dumb, you can rest assured knowing you're probably *at least* of average intelligence.

People learn through trial and error. That's called learning from your mistakes. That's a good way to learn, but learning through mistakes can lead to bankruptcy, crush your bones, or cause you to die. I've had my fair share of mistakes, many of them things I did physically, like executed dangerous flips, dives off of high platforms, or assaulting my liver and lungs with foreign substances until near failure. I was always a decent athlete, but I can't say I'm of high *Bodily-kinesthetic Intelligence*. Perhaps what it comes down to is being average, a word that elicits yawns.

I've done a lot of dumb things for someone who thinks he's smart. Looking back over my life, I'm shocked I'm still alive. Perhaps that's the problem. Smart people think they're dumb and dumb people think they're smart. If I do something stupid, I curse myself as an idiot. You'd hope the advantage of being smart is to stop yourself from doing something stupid before you execute the action, but that's not always the case. It's not such an easy thing to realize stupid things in the moment, because doing stupid things can take longer to figure out than expected. Smart people smoke all the time, even though they know it's killing them, and many people have romanced and married the wrong person, an act that can take years to complete, even though the signs of it being a horrible decision are as apparent as the words on this page.

I write books about my dumb decisions – a historical documentation of each questionable choice, set in words for posterity, and more or less, for people's entertainment – but perhaps it's so they can avoid the trappings of someone who is not smart in the "dictionary sense" of the word.

The Collector

I was cruising Craigslist looking for a fix, desperate to find something to fill the void. This was during Craigslist's glory days when you could coordinate strange and twisted sexual encounters with strange and twisted people, or, if you were so inclined, barter drugs with things like, say… oh, I don't know, maybe… Crest teeth-whitening strips. I know because I've done just that. Whitening strips are quite expensive. Nothing to sneeze at. I sold mine for a decent haul. He got a bright smile, and I got a bright day.

So, there I was scanning Craigslist, looking for something to satisfy my cravings. Filtering through keywords both targeted and with innuendo, when finally, I found something to satisfy my soul. A shot to the cranium… the nervous system… the void inside my chest.

40 vein-flooding beauties, still in the package, sure to give me exactly what I needed. I snapped at the keyboard, asking if they were still available, and was met with an instant

response.

"Yes, they're still available. Come get them now."

"Where are you located?" I pleaded, one foot out the apartment door.

"Tribecca."

Tribecca. Manhattan. Where the money is. The land of Wall Street bro fuck pads, secret movie star lairs, and old-world money invested in chef-style kitchens and Basquit art. Of course she was in Tribecca. That's where you always find the real good shit. Clean. Un-cut. Without the dirty fingers of middlemen manipulating the product.

When I arrived, the plump blonde girl couldn't have been more than 25. Her face said 21, but her attitude said 45. A scorned lover, she was standing in a half-empty apartment, selling off her cheating boyfriend's material possessions like a carnival barker for two cents on the dollar. She was going to SHOW HIM who was boss. She was going to show him not to fuck with her feelings… treat her like dirt… and all the other bullshit that comes from a girl having her first real-world punch in the chest.

She was with her friend, an Indian girl, who was enjoying the fire sale as much as her. Everything had to go, no matter what it was. Clothes, furniture… medicine.

It was a sunny Sunday afternoon, and the light poured into the one-bedroom apartment overlooking the park as the sun crept down over the west side of Manhattan. I asked her where *they* were, and she pointed to a box on the floor. I turned, got down on my knees and opened the large nondescript cardboard box in the naked corner of the room. The fix I needed. 40, mint-condition *Star Wars* action figures from the Power of the Force collection, still in their blister packs and meticulously packed in sheets of bubble wrap. I couldn't believe it. She wasn't lying. There they were… *all my old friends*; Leia, Chewbacca… C3PO. Every cardboard edge as tight as a drum, like they'd never left the factory.

I looked up at the girl and swallowed hard.

"Forty bucks?"

"Yeah, just give me forty. Serves him right."

The girls giggled with delight.

In the grand scheme of things, it didn't feel right. Sure, deal of the century, no doubt… but we *Star Wars* fans needed to stick together; right? Then, the rush came to my head knowing these babies would be mine and I forked over the 40.

The guilt trip lasted about 5 seconds.

"I'll take 'em"

"Get out of here fast."

I didn't argue, I was out the door and into a taxi before you could say Boba Fett with rocket launcher.

The two taxi rides across town and back were almost the price of what I paid for product itself. But the street market value, and the satisfaction of that score carried me through for quite some time. I pored over the collection for hours. Had each blister laid out on different flat surfaces over my tiny apartment. The couch, the arms of the couch, the ancient coffee table I got from my grandmother, and on my bed, which I'd shockingly made that morning.

I looked at each figure. Their clothing, their weapon of choice. IG-88 and his long blaster; Princess Leia and her stun gun, dressed in the original Star Wars film's long white gown with hood draped over the head; and Darth Vader, who for some reason was pressed into a particularly jacked-up He-Man mold in this series, looking like David Prose in his early body-building days.

Any collector knows the feeling of bringing a prized skin home from the wild – back to the safety of your house where the doors are locked and no one can take it away. The treasure is yours and the blood is spiked with endorphins and adrenaline.

I still had my Star Wars action figures from my childhood, frozen in the carbonite of time inside a closet at my parents' house. My parents were instructed to 'never throw anything out in my old closet.' A command they took to heart. They'd heard all the horror stories before. The mother who tossed 2 million bucks in baseball cards while her son was away at college. The comic books worth more than stock dumped in the dumpster so the parents could turn the upstairs into a TV room. Of course, there's always the tragedies too. The house fires, the devastating floods.

All my old figures were nestled tightly inside a plastic Darth Vader storage case along with a few speeder bikes, an AT-ST walker, and the Jabba the Hutt set, with his giggling sidekick Salacious Crumb. Although not in their precious blisters, still mint and handled gently, unlike my friends who buried theirs in the dirt to resurface millenia later by some new creature that roams the earth in the year 5188.

My Star Wars figures were safe. They sat in the closet with a footlocker filled with my most prized comic books, a collection I'd been curating since 1985, and my hand-held LCD video games, a collection I'd kept since I was 10.

The Power of the Force lot would be an excellent addition to my collection… a temporary satisfaction until the lingering creep of needing more crept into my soul. Again, the never-ending pursuit. The thrill of the hunt. Similar to the man who must conquer his quest to bed the woman, yet is not really interested in the long-term relationship. The collector is not satisfied to simply possess and rest. They must have more and more and more. But is it ever truly enough?

•••

The first thing I can remember collecting when I was a little kid was rabbit pelts. Don't ask why. It was the 1970s and people seemed to have a lot of rabbit pelts. Perhaps it was just my family and their immediate surroundings. It was a time shortly after Woodstock, when folks wore fringed leather vests, bellbottom jeans, giant belt buckles encrusted with Turquoise, and hair down to their waist. Rabbit pelts seemed like a natural extension of that. I think my maternal uncle Jim was the first to give me a rabbit pelt, then my paternal uncle Bill gave me another. Both, not surprisingly, attended the aforementioned Woodstock peace and love festival.

Later, I got another two rabbit pelts at an estate sale in my neighborhood. I remember it clearly. The people were selling everything in the house, so anyone could walk through and shop. The pelts were upstairs on their bed, and I purchased them for a few bucks. It was brave of me to enter that house because this couple had two vicious Doberman Pinschers, one black and one chocolate brown. These two sleek, shiny, laser-fast, hunt-down-and-maul-a-toddler-before-you-could-bat-an-eye killing machines terrorized a certain section of my neighborhood for years – directly across a vacant lot where my friends and I played baseball in relative peace. Maybe the Pinchers killed the two rabbits those pelts derived from. I don't know. But the dogs were not on premises the day of the sale. Maybe they were spilt up in the divorce.

I hung the rabbit pelts around my desk like they were trophies I'd hunted myself, along with actual sports trophies. The pelts made me sneeze because I was allergic to fuzzy, hairy things so my mother tossed them out.

The next thing I collected were pocketknives. My uncle Chip gave me a few from his junk drawer filled with cool things – mainly pocketknives. Pocket knives were another staple of the 1970s, as well as uncles who gave things away. On a winter trip to Maine visiting my Uncle Greg, we stayed at his uninsulated cabin where he kept his gargantuan record collection neatly organized in floor-to-ceiling built-in shelves. It was the sturdiest thing in the dump. On that trip, we camped out for the day inside L.L. Bean where I got my first real Swiss Army pocketknife. The classic red with two knives, bottle opener, screwdrivers, toothpick, corkscrew and the confusing awl/reamer/puncher, which no one has used for its intended purpose since 1891. That's the pointy thing that has a weird sharp edge, a "sewing needle" hole and dull front. It's great for unclogging your weed pipe, scraping residue from your weed pipe, and any other weed related tasks, but not for leather, or sewing, or anything else it's meant for.

As the 1980s rolled in, my first real collectable came to fruition, but not through my own obsession. Trains. My father and I built a train set in our basement after being gifted a set of used Marklin HO scale engines, box cars and tracks, which commenced a large-scale diorama project that went unfinished even after a decade+ of tinkering, gluing and painting. There's a scene in the film Goodfellas when Henry and Karen get married, and every attendee congratulates them by stuffing a wad of cash into their hands. There's so many envelopes, Karen becomes overwhelmed. That was me during Christmas 1980, except I was nine, and the money wads were wrapped boxes of trains. Word got out that I was building a train set and the family plundered every car and engine available at local hobby shops, which back in the day were plentiful. Every time I turned around, someone was stabbing a train box into my hand with a warm "Merry Christmas" and gentle pat on the head. I must have received 30 trains that year. It was ridiculous. I thought this would be my life forever, but once I hit puberty I was generally ignored until… well, now.

At some point, my family began giving everyone coins as holiday gifts. Especially the boys and men. If you watched any channel on television from 1980 through 1988, you were bound to see minute-long infomercial spots for collectable coins, all of them presented in felt boxes with official paperwork, minted in limited edition, guaranteeing these stunning, all-American collectors items would skyrocket in value. All 700,000 of them. Busts of our forefathers double-struck in glimmering silver and encased in hard plastic to protect the value spun across the screen while banners of the stars and stripes yet waved. No one gave much thought to these coins except for me because even at a young age, I equated collectables with appreciating prices. Because of everyone's indifference, I managed to accumulate their coins and amass a mini Fort Knox celebrating George Washington's birthday, America's war victories, and centennials here and all over the world. I suppose any reason is a good reason to mint a coin, and that's exactly what they did.

When I got a bit older, I collected toys, especially *Star Wars*. This collection arose mainly because I held onto all my toys over the years. I was one of those weird kids who kept their action figures in pristine condition while his friends blew the heads off their figures with firecrackers. Although I was fastidious in my nature with these items, I wasn't aware enough to keep them in their valuable blister packs and boxes, although I kept a few boxes for the larger vehicles and space-ships.

In the throes of collecting Star Wars trading cards, I naturally progressed to sports trading cards, mainly football. But my true collecting addiction didn't enter my veins until I was 13, where I found the passion that's relented only in physical form, but not for the art and culture – comic books. It was a fascination that engulfed 20 years of my life. In fact, my addiction was so deep, I fantasied about breaking into one of my favorite comic books shops and robbing it. My plan was to smash my Jeep Renegade through the front door, rip the valuable comics they had taped to the walls high above the register, then bolt before the cops came. Never mind the fact that they yanked a bolted metal gate down at closing time. Unfortunately, that place burned to the ground years later… I had nothing to do with it.

I would drive all over Long Island and visit every comic shop I knew about, digging and pilfering books from bins and stacks. I'd hit garage sales and church sales and even mothball-scented thrift shops to find lost treasures in the wild. I would often run across a tall guy named Chris who had the same idea. He quickly became my friend/nemisis. I'd roll into a shop and Chris would enter minutes later, snooping around to see what was recently brought in. His philosophy was to get as many first issues as he could. A good strategy. Mine was to get key issues featuring main characters that sprung up before they became iconic… Wolverine, Groo the Wanderer, The Punisher, and other costumed heroes and vigilantes. I'd collect artist and writer's early work before their work sky-rocketed them into the lexicon of fame.

For me, the collecting of comic books was not just a grouping of analogous pairings of sets. It was the calcu-lated hunting and gathering of rare art that satisfied some-thing inside my soul that required systematic order that could not, *would* not be quenched without completion. It can only be described as something more enigmatic than obsession. Not achievement or accomplishment… maybe an anal-retentive mania more in line with mathematical autism. A singular neurodivergent OCD focus that requires rule, structure and order. I spent years pawing over comics – finding versions in as mint condition as one could hope to get, carefully bag-ging them is fine acetone, backed firmly with acid free card-board, keeping the books pin straight and in new condition. I watched their value like stocks on the S&P 500. I would skip parties, gatherings with friends, and nights out on the town to procure comics so I could carefully read, bag and catalog them like a historian… a librarian of pop art masterpieces and their culture. This was not a sad and lonely existence. It was a lifestyle I relished and fell into absolutely – without regret, without apprehension.

Even today as I gray into someone's "old man" I become giddy at the sight of comic books. My eyes twirl like rainbow-swirled lollipops as I fawn over the art, style, cartoon bright colors and the unfolding storylines inside each calculated and designed panel.

•••

What is the obsession of collecting? Why do we do it? Are we natural pack animals that must collect things, or is there an inherent biological factor where *things* equal *value*? In relation to basic survival, it could mean value in terms of tradable items used for food, or other survival items that protect us from predators, the elements, or other humans. In modern settings, perhaps it's about appearances… prestige and hierarchy, as well as comfort and happiness.

Besides the collecting of tangible items like objects, there's the collection of memories or experiences. Scientists believe there's a strong correlation between, or perhaps more realistically, a fine line separating the hobby of continuum and serious mental disorder. Sigmund Freud introduced theories of psychosexual development and drive theory, man's need to satisfy negative forces with fulfillment by external needs, which if not met, will cause unsatisfied tension. Other psychoanalysts have identified five main motivations for collecting: for selfish purposes; for s*elfless* purposes; as preservation, restoration, history, and a sense of continuity; as financial investment, and as a form of addiction. The dark side of collecting has been shown to have hoarding tendencies.

However we approach the hobby of collecting, there's no doubt it gives a fulfillment not easily found in other hobbies or activities. Worldwide about 30% of people collect things. Most for healthy reasons. Small trinkets on the shelf make us happy because it's fun; people collect because they "like" certain animals, characters or people; or they found themselves with an abundance of one thing and felt compelled to get more. The dark side of collecting, other than hoarding, is to make oneself financially or mentally unstable by being a completist, when it's clearly impossible do so because there's a never-ending supply of the collectible material.

There's also the hunting and procuring of objects that have historical relevance. People become keepers of items that otherwise may be lost by the hands of time. Sometimes it's altruistic in nature... cataloging and documenting materials and the item's significance to the annals of time which makes them apart of the world as a whole. There's nostalgia aspects to collecting, competitiveness, recognition, social status, and control. If one can create a small world of order of their choosing, one can seek peace and relaxation in that place and add or subtract from it when necessary or when desired.

I'm not sure why I got into collecting. Maybe it's the feeling of having treasure – valuable things that equate to money. Like a pirate and their booty – a chest filled with gleaming gold and jewels. Perhaps it's the ownership of something rare – ownership of something where only a few exist in the world, putting me in an exclusive group. There's a feeling of having things that are desired by many, but not enough to go around. When the rare desirables are many and showcased in one place, they become trophies – hunted items in the wild exhibited as artifacts in a carefully curated gallery.

Mostly for me it was about nostalgia. As I got older, I was able to afford the things I didn't have. Although I had some, I didn't have them ALL. And that is the obsession with collecting… having them all. Sure, having every comic book ever made is absolutely impossible. You'd need to have space for millions of comics and absurd wealth to purchase them. But to have the BEST collection is a goal some achieve through a lifetime of work.

By the time I was 35, I had one of the biggest (and best) collections in the world of digital handheld LCD games. Exceeded by only one or two other people in the world – a man in Hong Kong and a man in Sweden. My obsession with these handheld games came late, but the seed that was planted started early. While rummaging through old boxes of toys and comics in my parent's attic, I discovered my old games from the early 1980s… a Sega tabletop Frogger game, a Tomy bowling wristwatch, a rare Enter Crazy Climber game, and a few Nintendo Game & Watch games – a duel screen Donkey Kong game, and a single screen Popeye game. When I saw them again, a lightning bolt zapped right through me and before I could think straight, I was on eBay scanning the airwaves for more.

These LCD handheld games were incredibly unique and fun to play. Most of them released in the early 1980s where their popularity soared before they tapered off in the mid-1980's, and then finally killed off when the Nintendo Gameboy was released in 1989. Although the single-game handheld LCD games continued into the early 1990s, mostly through Tiger Electronics, they were officially gone from the market by the mid 1990s with only a few stragglers coming out as nothing more than a cheap gift, or because the company had no other means to release a Gameboy competitor.

I eventually spread out and purchased everything related to handheld gaming. I bought the original Gameboy new in the box, as well as it's many incarnations over the years including Gameboy Pocket and Gameboy Color. Living in Manhattan, there were many vintage video game spots to dig for these items and their games. I secured something in the range of 500 unopened Gameboy games, some incredibly rare as these vintage game stores bought old stock and crammed them into every nook and cranny of their overstuffed shelves. I collected the games and consuls of Gameboy's main competitor, the Sega Game Gear. There were many rare consuls and games that came to the store shelves, mostly in Asia, where the handheld craze boomed like a virus. I collected those as well, and living a short walk from Chinatown in Manhattan, I hunted through the small catacombs of game stores for years, picking up rare items and lost treasures like Indiana Jones.

Although this was my single-minded focus for a solid seven years, I collected other things. Mainly first addition books and vinyl record albums. To fuel these collections, I began selling off my comic books, which netted me an amazing profit. Mostly because my comics were in pristine condition and desirable. I also sold my collectible coins, which netted me a decent price, but nothing more than what I expected from coins struck and sold by the warehouse full. I essentially traded one obsession for another. While this was happening, I began working for a toy design company, which then fueled my desire to continue to collect toys, mainly *Star Wars* toys and action figures, as well as other toys and action figures.

Pumping the adrenaline of every collector from San Francisco to Singapore was eBay, which started as a simple auction site called AuctionWeb in September 1995 and eventually became a massive cultural phenomenon, selling everything from vintage automobiles, Beanie Babies, Pez dispensers, to creepy ancient China Dolls. Every collector in the world flocked to the site to either sell their valuables, or obtain more. Nothing was off limits other than body parts, live animals, alcohol, bootlegged and counterfeit materials as well as a few others, but everything else was up for grabs. I was one of its biggest fans. I bought and sold so many items off the site, it became part of my DNA. Combined in hours, I spent literal months of my life on the site, searching up and down for essential pieces, as well as those gone under the radar when improperly cataloged by its unsuspecting seller.

•••

Before he was the terribly intimidating General Zod in *Superman II*, Terence Stamp was the terribly intimidating protagonist of the film *The Collector* (1965), which was about a strange man who collected butterflies, but wanted to collect humans, especially a woman who became the focus of his strange obsession. Like many collectors, his focus would not stop until he had what he wanted.

One of my favorite shows in the early 2000s was *The Incurable Collector*, hosted by John Larroquette, of *Night Court* fame. He was a sophisticated host who himself collected first edition books. The show featured people from all over the world and their unique and valuable collections, ranging from comic books and toys, to rooms full of banana-related items. In one episode, a couple were obsessed with Tiffany and Co. items and would virtually make themselves cash-poor to procure their treasures, admitting they reduced themselves to beans and rice for meals because of the item's cost.

This American Life has a wonderfully gripping episode called 'Feather Heist' where a young man named Edwin Rist, whose proclivity for tying beautiful flyfishing ties drove him to rob one of the world's most expensive and unique feather collection in the world, decimating years of rare feather collecting from extinct birds by scientific explorer Alfred Russel Wallace in his pursuit of tying the most beautiful fly ties he could. The repercussions of his actions had the opposite effect that drives most collectors to follow their collecting goals; instead of being a curator of items, Rist destroyed a part of history in his pursuit of creating another, devastating a branch of Ornithology lost in time forever. Although seemingly small in nature, this type of obsession is a prime example of the dark side of the hobby and obsession that is collecting.

As I was deep into my LCD game collection, my comic books were virtually gone. Back on Craigslist, I answered an ad for a man looking for vinyl records. Standing in my Manhattan bedroom, I fanned out my remaining records for display, mostly rare, but not incredibly rare. This man of perhaps middle eastern decent, looked certifiably insane as he stood drooling over my records. I believe I could have sold them for any price I wanted, but I was fair, and carefully described each record and its value, which he paid for without hesitation. Thinking back, he was rather unhinged and I had him standing in my actual bedroom, hovering over the bed I slept in, but I believe all he wanted was records, although he may have been bordering on mental disorder.

The collecting bug embedded itself so deep, I began collecting things outside of my passions. I placed notices in online forums for old comic books, toys, and candy store stock that was stored away… by business that went under, by owners who retired, or people who simply stored things away. Among the many mines I dug through, I sifted through a frail old man's brutally hot attic on Long Island, a back storage room at a record store in Philadelphia owned by a gruff black man with white beard stubble, and later, I dug into a storage unit in Queens opened by a slug of a woman who chain-smoked the entire time I rummaged. Those never produced the Eureka gold-mine moments I'd hoped, but through my digs I discovered and purchased boxes of unopened Wacky Packs (humorous trading cards and stickers of consumer products); 1970s Fleer baseball cards (still with their petrified pink bubble gum slabs inside); choice Golden Age DC comics (including early, yet well-handled Superman issues); Towers of sealed VHS tapes (Xtro and Xtro II!); Underground hip hop records (JT the Bigga Figga - Dewlin' in the Lab!); sealed action figures on cards (Ninja Turtles and The Iron Giant), and a host of other random things, most of them netting smaller and bigger prices than I imagined.

The amount of time and energy I devoted to this venture began to take its toll. My friend Mark, a world-traveler who collected everything from early American Silverware sets, textiles, and vintage pens, became a hostage to his collectibles. His babies were piled high, threatening to tumble onto his head with a fretting fear of losing them to selfish hands, or to unsuspecting back-stabbing colleagues. I realized I was essentially acquiring and losing things at the same rate; with not much gained or lost. Tangible items were nothing but a mist, and I found myself hustling to educate my brain to validate the value of every item I held, and every item strewn across every stupid garage sale and garbage pile. I tried identifying makers marks stamped into vases, paint work decals over old tin toys, famous names signed across oil paintings, and so many categories that to be even a *reasonable* semi-expert in these fields would require 10 lifetimes and multiple brains to gain their understanding... stained glass, vintage furniture, Bakelite jewelry, porcelain figures, posters, art, timepieces, guitars, guns, wine, ephemera, Beanie Babies...

I eventually succumbed to the fact that not only was I being weighed down by vast boxes filled with collectible items, but was hustling for treasure that would never truly satisfy my soul. Like Mark, it began to weigh on my mind until it was all I thought about. The art of the hustle took its toll, and I wondered what it all meant.

By the time my son was born, I'd sold every collectible I owned except for a handful of comic books worth nothing more than good art and stories. Over those collecting years, I spent more time at the post office, shipping items across the planet than just about anyone else short of a shipping factory... to the point where I knew the international postal system better than anyone else other than the post office staff itself. I released, like my little nurtured birds, something in the range of two thousand cardboard packages filled with rare comics, collectible coins, and vintage video games into the world. I sent things all over the United States as well as Germany, England, Egypt, Hong Kong, Japan, Australia, New Zealand, Brazil, Colombia, Canada, Finland, Spain, and parts of Northern Africa. I most likely netted and sold something in the range of a few hundred thousand dollars' worth of collectable items in that time. In the end I made a pretty tidy final sum; mainly because I educated myself on my collectible items, as well as had the patience to sell at the right time… the latter being a collector's Kryptonite. I miss the things I've collected over the years, but the memory of them is seared in my brain.

The cost of collecting is immense, both with time and with money... but it can cost you your heart as well. You can be emotionally attached to these things, and to sell them off, give them away, or lose them, can scoop out a piece of your soul that is not easily replaced. Once these items are gone, you realize they were holding you down. The fear you have in losing them or accidentally destroying them is immense. Finally being rid of them can be a huge relief.

My old boss once said to me (a boss who owned a tremendous amount of stuff), "You don't own your stuff, your stuff owns you." He was absolutely right. Your stuff begins to weigh you down. You don't physically carry these things on your back, but you might as well. They weigh heavily on your mind. You think about them, wonder about their condition, hope they're ok, and grow concerned if you haven't seen them in a while.

Collecting can be a deeply satisfying venture, but it can be wearisome as well. You can never truly be satisfied, so at times, it feels like you really shouldn't do it at all. You are only an item's owner for so long, until it's eventually in the possession of someone else.

As the old saying goes… "you can't take it with you."

Someone's Rocking
My Dreamboat

I live in a dream world. It's fascinating in there. Wonderful. A carefully constructed nirvana where things rarely go wrong. It's the place I go to be an important somebody. Dragon slayer, world traveler... a famous somebody. Not a famous person of anything particular, although, since I'm a writer it could be that profession. But in my dream world, the profession is not important. I just find myself on discussion panels and talk shows. People ask me questions because they want to know if I enjoy regular things, just like them, even though I'm wildly famous and important. How do I like my coffee? What am I currently reading? What are my top 10 films? Things that will make people even *more* intrigued by my secret life behind closed doors.

If you're like me, you believe you could have done just about any job you found interesting if only you'd put enough hours into its mastery... forensic scientist/detective, chess champion, MMA fighter (focused on ground and pound combat), sommelier, and Tango dancer.

Reality can be a punch in the face. Sometimes worse than the drastic shock of a full-frontal attack by a crazed fist, is when reality slowly creeps in, like an invasive species. Like the sound of an alarm clock that gently raises its pitch from quiet beep to full squawk until it annoys you from your warm, wonderful, sleeping dream.

Reality can be like that. It's a relentless campaign to completely bum me out. I'm often trying to escape – slide into my own personal DMs (dream modes) and find out what fantasy I have growing. I tend to leave a fantasy and return where I left off... continue the world I've manufactured with fake people, false surroundings, and unearned stature. I've returned days later to scientific debates where my expertise was needed; reappeared at the dais at Comic Con where my fellow cast members were grilled by fanboys about our latest project; and I've slipped under the bed covers where women of different races and sexual tastes were waiting for me so they could finish the task at hand.

Sometimes I go to my dreamworld without any preconceived expectations and my imagination *gives* me a profession or role. Real dreams happen when the brain files and stores the day's external input, but fantasies can be the same. You can fantasize about what you experienced during the day, especially with the people you meet.

Reality is the ultimate party pooper. Like the cops, it's constantly knocking on the door just as the party is getting started. You're knee deep in a wonderful fantasy and before you know it, life is pulling you out of your little Cloud 9. Like the parents coming home early from vacation just as the boys are showing up with the keg. It's the ultimate kick in the balls.

Reality comes in so many forms. Your parents, your spouse, your kids, and of course, your job. Nothing says reality like sitting in the hard chair of a government building, waiting in line to hand someone paperwork so they can dispense a healthy dose of reality into your veins. They may force you to pay taxes, register a vehicle, judge another person in a court of law, or file papers so you can separate yourself legally from another human being.

These are the places I need to escape from. Sure, we have gardens and playgrounds in real life, but I can go to the world's greatest gardens and play on jungle gyms that tower into the sky – and I don't even need to get in a car to get there. I'll play on the sandy beach of my imagination while some old man coughs up a lung next to me at the doctor's office.

My wife loves to ask me, "What are you thinking?" Like I'm actually going to tell her.

"I'm thinking I've made a grave error on most of my life's decisions."

Is that what she wants to hear?

Usually when she asks me 'what I'm thinking' I'm doing something stupid like trying to figure out who had the most rebounds during the 1999 NBA season, but she wants to hear something more profound, like how much I love her and our son... which I do, but I'm usually not thinking about that when she asks. When I stare into space and she's curious as to what universe I've escaped to and asks: "What are you thinking?" I'm usually thinking about something mundane, like what meat I'm going to toss on the grill; or why I didn't ask for a raise last year; or how much money could I have gotten for those hubcaps I stole in high school; or what my reasoning was for turning down John Dilworth's offer to work on his animated show *Courage the Cowardly Dog*, a decision that would have changed the trajectory of my life.

Sometimes I'll stare off into space because I'm in a completely different universe. I've escaped to a fantasy land so I can sooth my soul and protect myself from the crushing reality of the brutal and heartless existence I reside in every day. The place that continuously crushes my dreams and spirits by the quarter hour. The depressing world that wants nothing to do with my ideas, creative thoughts, our brilliant concepts. I'm constantly on a mission to escape that place… that harsh reality that kills people by the second. Not from disease, or famine, or cancer or car crashes, but through a series of systematic bloodlettings that drain us of our identity until we're nothing but a social security number and a paycheck stub.

I'd like to take my wife along for this sentimental journey inward, but there's only room for one on the ride. One seat. One window.

If my wife had her way, she would be able to read my mind. I don't find that gift particularly illuminating. I don't care what anyone else is thinking. I have enough thoughts of my own. And if it's all the same to you and anyone else, I'd like to keep them that way.

This seems like a bold statement from someone who writes about their life. Someone who displays their inner thoughts and feeling in memoirs. But certain corners of my mind are off limits. Especially the utopias I've built in the outer reaches of my mind. These places have their own streets, road-side attractions, amusements parks, strip clubs, candy shops, drinking holes, drug dens and laws. The habitants are people that worship me, follow me around and are ready to do my bidding, or at the very least, interested in making me their leader so I can dictate my philosophies upon them. Powerful dictator is great, but what about beloved leader? A holy man that can change the world. Ruling with an iron fist seems cold and heartless. Killing people with kindness seems like the way to go.

I get mildly annoyed when someone inadvertently interrupts me while reading, watching a movie, listening to music, or having a conversation. But, when someone invades my dream, I become downright irate. Almost ferocious. "What the hell do you want?!" I bark.

"You want potatoes or rice?"

"Rice please."

Rice.

The giant hands of life reached in and yanked me through the fog… out of The Zone, away from the warm blanket of tender caresses, back to reality to be asked about a side dish… or homework… or the email someone sent… or why the house is on fire. Trivial things that have nothing to do with my carefully constructed dreamworld.

•••

I envy people locked in institutions. Not because the place is cozy. If anything, it's a nightmare of craven insanity. But the people there more or less have no idea because they're "off the grid" mentally. Checked out. Not capable of living in this time or place, or in any kind of reality.

Isn't that wonderful?

I envy them. Living in an alternate reality where anything can be going on. Sure, some of them are tortured souls who see nothing but horror 24/7, but many are living in simple worlds where taxes, rent, bills and other life inconveniences don't exist.

The other day I was going to work, entranced in my dreamworld as I took the stage at a rock concert, leading a crowd in a sing-along while my bandmates plowed through drum and guitar solos that would melt every face. Little did I realize I was doing 55 in a 30 and got pulled over by a law enforcement officer. Talk about the law shutting down the show. It was like the fire Marshall pulling the amp plugs for capacity violations.

The cop came to my window and asked if I knew how fast I was going? Of course I didn't know! I was performing at a rock concert! But I feigned ignorance and said, "38?" He said I was *going 55 in a 30.* He was very disappointed in me. Usually, I have a speech ready in my head for police officers if they pull me over asking if I knew if I was speeding.

"Of course I knew I was speeding! Everyone speeds," I'll shout. "If we didn't speed constantly, all day long, nobody would get anywhere. The speed limits have been the same since the day they invented cars. They haven't changed in 90 years! They're completely antiquated!"

When *this* cop came to the window, he asked me questions about my speed, and I acted like the fucking passive sheep I am. "Yes, sir and no, sir." I assume if I act like a dick, he'll give me the maximum fine in the State of New York and that's $30,000 or something like that. You need to mortgage your home to pay it off. After he handed me the ticket, the rock concert was officially over. It was a reunion tour too! A bunch of top-notch 1990s acts like Stone Temple Pilots and Pearl Jam. Very disappointing.

The ticket indicated I could either write in a plea, or go to their website and file a plea. The site didn't allow a plea of guilty, which I thought was odd, so I wrote guilty on the slip and mailed it in by snail mail. Apparently, I was supposed to plead NOT guilty and have a prosecutor defend my case. I figured, if the court noticed that I pleaded guilty, they'd mark me as a fine, upstanding citizen who takes responsibility for their careless actions. That was not the case. They mailed me a letter which basically said, "Get your ass the traffic court."

So, I went to traffic court to tidy up the mess I made. Talk about reality. Sure to kick one in the crotch like a wrecking ball. I showed up at court on a drizzly winter day and entered the joyless, brutalist cement-block building. I figured it would be a nightmare of poor folks wringing their hats in their hands, begging to be set free, not having any money to give to the New York State traffic machine, but it was a mix of all sorts of folks from all walks of life. Mexicans who got pulled for inspections, white women pulled for no registration, elderly men without license plates, and a smattering of people who were flying through construction zones because they were late, having spent the previous night drinking straight vodka, dreading the coming workday.

My ticket was reduced to an axe murder and was given a slap on the wrist. I'm kidding. It was reduced to an aggressive parking ticket, and I paid something slightly less than $30,000... but not by much!

Having liberated myself from the clutches of government oppression, I was free to return to my regularly scheduled dreamworld. To fully emerge oneself into a dream world, you must go all the way. If not, you're only on the edge of dreams, having one eye open for invaders, and it's not the same as a deep dive into pure fantasy.

I exited the municipal parking lot and headed to work. I was coasting down the road, driving the speed limit and mindful of getting a repeat pull-over by some crazed police officer trying to make a ticket quota so his superiors didn't toss him in a cell with a bunch of tattooed killers and rapists. Without realizing it, the reduced speed limit lulled me into a comfortable place where I was free to dream again. My fantasy portal open and ready for me to drive into the place where I was wildly popular. So popular, in fact, I hosted the Academy Awards. The Academy was in a tight spot and asked me to jump in when the other hosts couldn't fulfill their duties – two hours before the curtain opened. It would be complete improv on my part, without the aid of the Academy's joke-bit army… a crew of some of the best gag writers Hollywood can fit into a room. I'd wear a tux by some new fashion designer, maybe an outfit by a woman who came in third on *Project Runway*, or that cheeky glass blowing show *Blown Away*, and dazzle the crowd with my charm.

Of course, I'd be a huge hit, which would rocket me to a level of stardom much higher than I had *before* I did the Oscars… if that's even possible.

Organ Donor

I once applied to be a sperm donor.

I was that hard up for cash.

My reason for donating sperm was nothing more than monetary. At the time I thought about what I could give the world that was worth anything, and the only things available were attached to me in solid or liquid form. I could have donated a kidney, but I needed both at the time. The way I drank, they were half polluted anyway. I like to keep my body parts in case someone I love needs them. Besides, I'd probably blow through the cash in a month and curse myself for having only one kidney with nothing to show for it except a worthless item I purchased online. Impulse purchase control is surely a criterion these donation places want in a human, and I don't believe I had that at the time, etching a mark against me right off the bat.

Regardless of what you think of your body, donating body parts must be an incredibly difficult decision outside of saving a loved one. Filmmaker Robert Rodriquez funded his first film *El Mariachi* after using the money he earned donating his body to science experiments. If that's not dedication, I don't know what is. The man could have exited the laboratory with an extra arm or with radioactive sperm, making him sterile. It's possible he could have gotten some awesome superpower, but that's doubtful. These lab people are either looking for a way to cure people of cancer, or to destroy them with the toxic poisons we spread on our food and children's toys. It's frightening. 35+ years later, Robert is still with us and has healthy children, so all is good.

My uncle Bill essentially did the same thing as Robert Rodriquez. He was a wonderful artist and painter, but had terrible cancer and donated his body to a lab group in exchange for an experimental cancer treatment and some funding to live, which extended his life a few years. One of the criteria for this treatment was to wear clothing with drug logos on them. One family gathering, he came dressed in a fashionable wind-breaker jacket, pants and ball cap with the Viagra logo twisting around him like he stepped out of the winning Indy 500 race car.

Science experiments on my body was not a route I could go. Comedian George Lopez got a kidney from his wife. Then he divorced her. One can only hope she was well compensated from the parting of both their union *and* her kidney. Melissa Etheridge, the renowned lesbian folk rock musician, had children through the sperm donation of famous rock legend David Crosby, tossing into the wind the fact that he was a raging alcoholic who himself needed a liver transplant. Oh, the irony. Unfortunately, Crosby and Etheridge's son Beckett died from an overdose of opioids, showing that sometimes the apple doesn't fall far from the tree. Apparently, Mr. Crosby donated sperm to heterosexual women for many years the old-fashioned way – the blow and go method. I think they're still tabbing up the numbers.

Ego seems to be a driving force for people to become sperm donors. They're convinced they're so damn wonderful, there should be more of them walking around. All the dashing good looks and clever thoughts, without having to raise the sticky brats themselves. I'm not sure how it works these days with all the genetic testing going on – perhaps you sign a waiver claiming never to take one. I suppose if you donated a few gallons of the stuff, you could have a whole colony of kids running around, and if they all search to meet you, they may discover you're the certifiable sociopathic asshole we all think you probably are. Your name and address are probably online for all to see – along with your family tree, and a world map of where your genetic DNA sprang from, making you who you are.

I read a story about a doctor who used his own sperm to impregnate about 30-something women who all had children who looked exactly like him. All a bunch of chubby, freckled, read-headed rug rats. No offense to read heads, but I don't think even red headed women want a sperm donor to be a red head. They can't sit anywhere exposed to the blazing sun and are generally considered to have the least attractive coloring among humans. The worst insult you can give someone is to call them a red-headed stepchild. That should say it all. This doctor inseminated all these women, who had a brood of portly little doctors. At least he was a doctor, a profession that shows signs of high intelligence, except *this* doctor lost his license for being a dumbass who impregnated multiple women, which was illegal. Perhaps that cancelled out the "being a doctor" part.

There are certain men addicted to getting women pregnant. TV host Nick Canon has impregnated so many women, he needs a personal secretary to remind him of his children's names. Hopefully the secretary is a man, because if they're a woman, he'll impregnate her too. Nick is donating sperm like a madman, yet getting none of the benefits of anonymity. Nick will need to work three lifetimes to pay for all these kids to grow up. Maybe the first kid can get a job ASAP – keep that money chain going down the line.

Blood is a common denotable body liquid. I'm unable to give blood because I have a fear of needles. I get woozy just thinking about it. I can watch a movie where people are blown to pieces as the hero wades through a river of blood, but pull out a needle and the color clears from my face while my heart rate drops to four beats per minute. At the time I was contemplating donating sperm, I was also frighteningly skinny, and a pint of blood would remove about a tenth of my body weight, so I passed on that choice. Not only that, people donate blood for free, their only reward being a cup of juice where they rip the foil lid off the top, and a few stale grocery store cookies. Why would they pay for something people are giving away for free? You could say the same thing about sperm. Dress up and swivel your ass on any barstool in Manhattan and you'll have donors lined up around the block. No, they haven't been vetted, and may be swarming with vile diseases and family histories consisting of every kind of cancer ever diagnosed, but those are the chances you must take. Although, if you're looking for a sperm donor, you probably have *some* personal morality, and the guy with five teeth sucking down his sixth noon beer at the honky-tonk is probably not it.

The whole process must be incredibly difficult for women. God only knows what maniac fluid you're sticking into your uterus. Sure, you can milk a nice batch of male gamete protozoa from a respectable man, but serial killers come around occasionally, and who knows how many generations it skips. For every Leonardo Di Vinci, Paul McCartney and Albert Einstein, there's some guy waiting in the shadows to eat a human liver with a wooden spoon. Most people are selfish, lazy, egotistic dolts. It's hard to skim that genius cream if it ever does rise to the top. If you think about it, the men who are donating sperm are kind of creepy. Who wants a kid whose father is that kind of sick, twisted bastard?

I decided that sperm was the way to go for my money issues regardless of any existential feelings about life, paternity and procreation. It doesn't take much sperm to solve the issue, it's easy to access, and not only that, I was constantly depositing it anyway; so why not get paid to jerk off? It's the thought process of a desperate man.

I went to a website for sperm donors and filled out the necessary form. I don't remember every question, but they do ask about your height, weight, what you do for a living, education level, and other questions you're assured to fail. I'm sure if you're a 6'4" Harvard medical grad with thick black hair and a 12-inch cock, they stamp the approval before it hits their inbox, but a skinny six-foot blond with a Syracuse University degree employed as a "designer" is met with a electric sigh. It's a good thing I didn't put writer as my employment, because that's guaranteed to make any children I bare unemployable, no offense to my son, who still has plenty of time to turn things around, although he's twice as intelligent than I was at his age. These sperm collectors are looking for genetic lottery winners – an army of studs that will wipe out the rest of the human race… or guaranteed to be first in line on the spaceship to salvation when the earth is doomed to die out, only to return later and repopulate the earth. Sounds like a dystopian novel, but these plans are being set in motion right now and you don't even know it.

I don't remember the name of the website. The internet was still in its development stages, so it's possible I gave valuable information to the Russians, some pervert in Asia, or on some database that will be used to steal my identity. Whatever the case may be, I hit send and waited idly by the computer for a response. In two days, I had it, and to my utter dismay, I was turned down. To be frank, I was insulted. How could they not want *this* I thought, looking over myself in a sweatshirt splashed with unidentifiable stains and jeans that could potentially walk on their own. They don't know what they're missing! It's the inner ramblings of someone who thinks they're far more superior than they are. Someone whose genius *and* talent has yet to be discovered. Someone who offers nothing other than mid-level sperm… again, no offense to my son, who's a straight-A student, a good basketball player and golfer, and is far better looking than I ever was. Perhaps that's the genes of my wife. Considering our struggles with money, she could donate her eggs. That's a different website. No masturbation required.

Blackout Drunk

When the electricity goes out, people groan like they've lost a helium balloon to the sky. There's no Wi-Fi, cable TV, or anything glowing in front of your face except candles. After an hour of silence in the dark, you wonder how humans enjoyed anything before electricity was invented. Sure, there's board games and talking, but what we really need is to be mainlined ASAP into the vein of interactive connectivity. Without it, borderline depression sets in.

On August 14, 2003, New York City experienced a blackout that plunged the entire city back to the year 1881. Permanent midnight. The bright lights of Broadway extinguished. Airplanes grounded. The Statue of Liberty, off duty. This event was not exclusive to New York City. A large chunk of the American Northeast went dark including Ohio and Michigan, as well as parts of Canada. A big 'ole chunk of North America.

Apparently, someone plugged a rusty toaster into a

faulty outlet in Cincinnati, and half the planet went blank. I'm kidding, but it did have something to do with Ohio.

Fucking Ohio.

People make fun of Cleveland, but have they ever been to Cincinnati? The place is a shit hole. At least it was a shit hole when I was there. That was a long time ago, but shit holes rarely make an about-face into glorious gardens.

The Buckeye State is where many great and terrible things derive. It's where Canton houses the Nation Football League's Hall of Fame, but it's also infamous for possessing the Cuyahoga River, a river that actually caught on fire. Yes, a river that contains water, caught on fire. Buckeyes, in case you didn't know, are tree nuts, which are plentiful throughout the area, but are inedible... so... that's Ohio in a nutshell... no pun intended.

Like I said, Ohio actually *was* the cause of the great and "terrifying" blackout. A computer bug did something or other to a grid... maybe insulted it, which caused one of the largest electrical blackouts in human history. I use quotes around terrifying because the news immediately latched onto the terror aspect of the story – projecting tyrannical sprees of looting and crime – roaming packs of brutes with baseball bats and pistols ready to rape the owners of every store while opening the skulls of children for laughs. The truth was, it was a hot night in the city, and it gave everyone an excellent excuse to have a three-day weekend so we could all chill out with our beer and fuck the hell off. If you were lucky enough to grab some beer. Which I did.

Initially, there were many pluses and minuses to the event. Many people had to walk home from work because the subway didn't run. I was lucky enough to be unemployed and didn't have to walk *anywhere* but to the nearest bodega to buy ice-cold beer before a major run on every fridge from Chinatown to Yankee Stadium occurred by the warm working class.

The only inconvenience I had that evening was waiting for my friends and neighbors to return from work. I was bored out of my mind. I sketched in my drawing pad while the car traffic slowly dissipated until there was none. Cell phones weren't working well, if at all, so I sat back and waited on my stoop, nibbling on a bottle of fermented hops from Seattle, hoping my friends used their power of deduction to know I was completely unencumbered by employment and free to hit the beer aisle the second the power flipped off, and would be there waiting for them like a beacon of hope.

That theory came true almost immediately. Before the sun dropped on 9th Street and Second Avenue, friends appeared from blurry clusters of people like magicians parting dense clouds of fog. By dinnertime, the streets were thick with humans, aimlessly wandering the avenues like a joyous and well-controlled apocalypse. An eerie energy filled the air because there was a real sense of potential anarchy. This was a city still stung by the ghost of 9/11. Folks were on good behavior, more or less, and still shell-shocked – but a stray beer bottle to the head or a swift kick in the nuts could sway a mob in any violent direction. People may pick a side whether there was a side to pick or not.

What really made it strange was the logistics of it all. When forced to use the stilted and boring sidewalk for your pedestrian transpiration, you become accustomed to a certain way of life. When you're given the option to walk in areas

reserved for 18-wheelers that rumble like out-of-control car-
go container, you get a strange sense of being out of your
element. Like, "Hey, I've never stood on *this* spot on First
Avenue for 20 minutes before. Kinda nice!" You can't help
but occasionally spin around and look for a taxi to mow you
down. By night, the city was nothing but foot traffic. Large
beds of people moved like clusters of gray amoebas squishing
along against a backdrop of pure black.

By the time 10pm rolled around, it was hard to see
your hand in front of your face. Between the drinking and the
smoking and the pitch blackness, and the fact smartphones
didn't exist yet, and no one in Manhattan owned a flashlight,
people were almost indistinguishable from one another. At
least from where my friends and I were standing. Packed
tightly in small rows of storefronts, not much light creeps
down those small one-way streets of the East Village. You realize New York City is almost completely worthless without
electricity. It's a dark, creepy, cluster of concrete that offers
nothing but shade… even at night. I talk shit about Cincinnati,
but New York City is a garbage strike and a rainstorm away
from being the world's *biggest* shithole. You can be strolling
down a beautiful block, cross the street and suddenly you're
on skid fucking row. The electricity may be the only thing
worth a damn in the whole worthless concrete jungle.

More impressive than my early beer grab, was the
number of makeshift bar-b-ques that sparked-up on the streets.
Sure, city dwellers don't own flashlights, but they're absolutely ready for impromptu grill sessions. I was handed my fair
share of burgers and random foods. The belief, I assume, was
that all the food would go bad without electricity; so why not

toss it over a fire and fatten up before the roaming packs of blood-thirsty motorcycle gangs commenced the skull-splittings like a Mad Max movie?

Eventually, the motorcycle gangs *did* appear. A pack of motorcycles rumbled up First Avenue, splitting the calm night air with brain-rattling engine blasts that seemed to go on forever. They came in endless waves. Just when I couldn't believe any more bikes would rumble up the avenue, more came. They came in chunks of 40, 50, 100 at a time. Rice burners, Harleys, mopeds, ATVs and Vespas. And when I thought more couldn't possibly come – more came. And more. And MORE. Guys flying by doing wheelies, people wrapped in Christmas lights, black kids with German WWII helmets, kids no more than 12 on ATVs, and daredevils surfing by, hanging ten on a Kawasaki doing 80 miles an hour. I'm not sure how they coordinated such a massive bike launch. They blasted through without stopping for what seemed like 20 minutes... and then they were gone. The air silent again with nothing more than the ring of laughter and the occasional shriek or whoop.

My apartment on the fourth-floor walk-up was used as the communal bathroom, and for some reason, the cooking station. The gas burners worked so cooking took place. At one point I went up, and my buddy Jen was whipping up noodles or something. The apartment was 800 degrees. Jen was a chef. Her entire family are chefs. Her father was a chef, and her brother was a chef. Her father owned a popular restaurant in L.A. Her brother was a personal chef to the stars. One time we went to the Hamptons with her brother, and he made beans at a cookout. I was like "We're in the Hampton's eating beans?" Then I was served the beans, and they were the best fucking beans I ever had in my life. Life-changing beans. I said, "These are the best fucking beans I ever had!" I still talk about those beans. So, if Jen was cooking, everyone was eating. It was a treat. The stiff night air was debilitating, but in my minuscule apartment it was like walking through fresh oatmeal. The endless walk up and down the stairs didn't help the body temperature either. Nor the heart-pumping alcohol intake. By the time I reached my apartment to empty my bladder, my legs were sweating and my legs *never* sweat. The noodles were excellent of course. We ate them on the stoop because the apartment was too dark and claustrophobic and candles made it even hotter, which seemed impossible, but they did. I knew sleep would be out of the question that night.

When the world shuts down, it's human nature to wander, sort of like the buffalo that roamed the plains, looking for water or fresh grass to chew. My crew and I started a concrete walkabout sometime around 11:00pm. It's amazing how quickly adults become children when unplugged and untethered from the world's umbilical cord. We were unable to make phone calls, make contact, nor cry for help. It's a child-like sense of whimsy to be that free, but it's also a feeling you get when you feel like the world is ending. Every man for himself. At least the 24 to 48 hour window when the electricity is out. You know it will go back to normal, but you should look for things to ration or to use as your apocalyptic outfit. Something like football shoulder pads, a top hat, maybe fishnet stockings with knee pads. Plus, a backpack or purse to store your cans of corned beef hash. Other accessories include: steel-toed combat boots, switchblade knife, fingerless leather gloves, mohawk, face paint, studded belt, brass-knuckles, crossbow and if you're so inclined… assless chaps.

Eventually we made our way to my local hangout, a bar on 4th Street and Second Avenue called BAR. Brothers Paul and Mike were pouring shots and handing them out to anyone who was interested in handing them money in return. We stopped for a few hits of Jamison whiskey... and that was all I remember from the night.

The next thing I knew, it was morning and my alarm went off at 7:30, except it was actually 10:15. I was in bed, twisted in a knot of sweaty sheets and for some reason, vinyl records, even though I didn't have a record player, nor the electricity to listen to them even if I did. Somewhere along the way, the electricity retuned and with it, the feeling of crushing oppression.

There were flashes of recollection as the day went on… skateboards and guitars in Washington Square Park; a girl handing out flowers at her flower shop; and, if I'm not mistaken, someone handed me an entire grilled steak, which I ate like a bagel.

Manhattan, the city that never sleeps and runs like clockwork regardless of what is happening, was set back a day like a time machine. My phone was free of messages, and everyone continued to pretend the world was blacked-out while hiding under the bedcovers until we sobered up, and realized everything was A-OK. We'd figure it all out on Monday. Those employed or not.

The rusty toaster in Cincinnati was tossed, some engineering nerd flipped a giant switch, and the electricity came back to our outlets and cable wires – righting the wrong that happened in Ohio and across the land – or, depending on how you look at it, wronging the right of a magical night where freak drinkers, endless motorcycle gangs, and freedom loving umbilical cord-cutters everywhere found a temporary utopia; a small urban playground where drunks, idiots, and full-grown children found a reason to escape their miserable lives and experience the end of the world. If only for one night.

In The Hospital

I just got out of the hospital. I hadn't felt well all week... headaches, vertigo and an overall feeling of shit. I was at work on Thursday, ate a plum, and about ten minutes later, felt nauseous, started hallucinating and almost passed out. Sounds more fun than it was. Friday, I couldn't get out of bed – called in sick. I went to urgent care, but the doctors gave me no drugs, or anything useful other than a list of disturbing and potentially crippling maladies which gave me a borderline anxiety attack. An hour later, I was in the hospital after I'd convinced myself I had anything from meningitis, heart failure, to some mysterious plum allergy.

Everyone I spoke to, mostly family and friends, had their own "professional" diagnosis... West Nile Virus, Lyme's Disease, Labyrinthitis, Covid, *Long* Covid, Strep Throat, allergies, exhaustion, and my father even suggested I get tested for cancer. That suggestion *definitely* calmed my anxiety.

I never go to the hospital. I hate the hospital. So my

decision to go did not come lightly. I felt like pure poop, so I went. Later in the process, the nurse asked me if I still lived on some street in Manhattan, seven living spaces prior, and miles from where I was currently sitting with tubes in me – over 20 years later. It made me think about my history of hospital visits.

The first time I was in the hospital, like many people, was when I was born. Some people are born in bathtubs at their house, in city cabs, in line at the grocery store, and unfortunately in filthy public toilets. The day I was born, my father had just hunkered down at work with a soggy tuna fish sandwich when he got a call that his wife was going into labor. After what "seemed like a month" according to my mother, I was born on the north shore of eastern Long Island on Monday, November 8th in what Hunter S. Thompson called "The foul year of our lord" …1971. On that day, Richard Nixon was the president, Led Zeppelin released their 4th album: the self-titled *Led Zeppelin* (aka ZoSo) and *The Exorcist* was the most popular book. People who share my birthday are Bram Stoker, Milton Bradley and Gordon Ramsey. Imagine chicken wings and cocktails on the back deck with *them*.

I was six on my second hospital visit. I had a fever and while my mother was taking my temperature with a mercury-filled glass thermometer, I accidentally crunched it in my mouth like a thin candy cane… like after you've sucked the thing for an hour into the shape of an icepick weapon. Usually, they put the glass thermometers in a kid's butt, but my parents went for the easier and more agreeable mouth entry. Of course, my parents flipped out, got all the glass bits off my tongue, and rushed me to the hospital's emergency room. There, we sat for hours in the hallway of a frenetic, over-stuffed ER while my mother pleaded for a doctor to look at her son. After a small eternity, a rushing doctor with a clipboard stopped, stooped over, and looked at me. He said: "eh, if Mercury had entered your son's blood stream, he be dead already." Then he rushed off to something far more important. We got up and left. I believe that was their plan all along; to see if I dropped dead and then say: "Yup, he had mercury poisoning!"

I'm not sure there's anything you can do about mercury poisoning anyway. It either kills you quickly, or turns you into a mutant with superpowers. Maybe there's a third option where mercury simply makes you nuts. Now that I think about it, it may have made me nuts.

The next time I entered the hospital after birth and the thermometer crunch incident, was when I was nine and got pneumonia. I'm not sure how I got it, or what the process of getting me to the hospital was. I don't remember anyone saying: "Holy shit, this kid has pneumonia, get him to the hospital!" I was suddenly in the hospital. I was just there. I remember that part very well. I was in a room with boy named Leslie who was about four, and Leslie screamed bloody murder day and night all four nights I was there. Needless to say, I got very little rest.

What made the experience incredibly surreal was the fact that I was in an oxygen tent most of the time. It was a wrinkled, soft plastic cube that covered me from the waist up, and everyone who walked past was a blurry mosaic painting. With sleep deprivation and high levels of oxygen pumped in,

I basically hallucinated. It might be where I got my affinity for mind-altering drugs. Adding to the mania was the TV. Mounted high on the wall, the small color set was either screaming cartoons, or droning on endlessly with something of little to no interest. I begged the nurses to turn it off, but Leslie wanted it on day and night and it drove me insane. I'd buzz the nurses to come turn it off, but the nurses were few and far between. Litteral ghosts. I recovered in an abandoned hospital. This was the hospital system of the 1970s, where doctors smoked cigarettes in your face and a patient could get a staph infection by simply looking at the walls.

The food was absolutely atrocious. I was a picky kid, no doubt, but this was medieval food. Viking food. At one point I was served watery eggs and liquid rice and went on a hunger strike. This is where the reputation of hospital food took hold. It's improved slightly today, but back the 1970s and 1980s, it was the kind of glistening slop that caused prison riots. It drove people to murder or go on that diet they'd been meaning to start for a decade. The people preparing the food were drunken malcontents from prison work release programs who lived in cardboard boxes. They had one arm and wooden teeth. They'd killed and maimed for pocket change and even *they* wouldn't eat that shit. One is supposed eat to maintain strength during recovery, but hospital food makes airplane food resemble a billionaire's chef-prepared dinner aboard their 200-foot yacht.

At one point I was so weak, I needed the help of both a nurse and my mother to walk me to the bathroom to pee, which fortunately was right across the hall. I don't think I crapped once during my stay. I took a few trips up and down the hallway to get my legs back, and was able to say hello to the nurses at the nurse station, all of them strangers as they'd ignored me the entire time I was there.

The only joy I found in the madness were the cards my classmates made. On my last day, having finally escaped the oxygen tent, I read all the funny cards everyone drew for me. They were pencil and crayon drawings of me in the hospital, me standing on baseball pitcher's mound (not my position), and pictures of dogs and sunny days walking on the grass. They said, 'get well soon' and a few even said, 'I love you.' Two days later I was playing in a blizzard, which I'm sure gave my mother a borderline heart attack.

Whenever one goes to the Emergency Room, they go because they have unknown pain, uncontrolled nausea, or their arm is missing. Unfortunately, whether it's full-blown trauma or a tiny fever, they'll spend the better part of a day in the emergency room – and probably the night as well. I've never gone to the hospital as a patient or with the sick person and spent *less* than 8 hours there. Now I know why husbands toss a bag over their shoulder when taking their pregnant wives to the hospital when *it's time*. It's not for the wives. The wives will be wearing a gown for three days. The bag is for the husband. It's filled with snacks, games, puzzles, cell phone, sketch pad, tax forms, and their entire Miles Davis Jazz collection. Enough to occupy them for a least a few hours. People should go to the Emergency room with the same bag.

My next hospital visit was when I was 31. I had a full mental breakdown, thought I was having a heart attack, and checked myself in. It's amazing I went over 20 years without an emergency room visit. None of my dumb friends ever jumped off a roof and broke their leg. No one was shot (or shot me), which says a lot with the number of guns we shot. No one broke their head open or was in a terrible car wreck. We used to throw knives at one another and knock them away with nunchucks, and launch fist-sized rocks straight into the air with tennis rackets to see where they'd fall, but we remained death-free. How, is a mystery.

I broke both my wrists in school; once when I was hacked across the arm in a lacrosse game, the other the following year when I fell in Volleyball. I went to spike the ball, got my feet tangled under the net with the opponent trying to block it, and we both fell backwards – and *crack*. Fell on my hand. I've hurt myself bending my neck to eat a taco, blew out my shoulder fishing for keys under my car seat, hurt my spine hiccupping, and got a concussion when I fell in a bar when I was black-out drunk. None of those things sent me to the hospital. An anxiety attack finally did.

•••

I just got back from the doctor. I had a follow up with my general practitioner after being in the hospital. I don't like doctor's offices, but at least it's not the emergency room. My doctor looked me over and said I was fine. He assured me it wasn't Lyme's Disease.

"You'd be even sicker if you had Lyme's Disease."

He also assured me it wasn't West Nile Virus.

"Even if it was, we couldn't do anything about it."

That's my kind of disease – the one you can't do anything about. At least there's no work involved; chipping away at my precious time. "I have West Nile Virus? Fuck it, let's go to the beach."

He diagnosed me with Vertigo, which may have been brought on by a small ear infection, or something like that. Ciao ciao bambino. I was out of my doctor's office in about five minutes. It was wonderful. I was back in my car listening to Captain Beefheart's *Trout Mask Replica* because I'm trying to get through Rolling Stone Magazine's *500 Greatest Albums of All Time* and that's on the list, even though it sounds like a bunch of 14 year-old deaf-mutes picked up instruments for the first time, and played the album while rolling down a hill in garbage cans. Still, there was a sense of beauty to the album because I was free from doctors.

Most people loathe doctors' offices and emergency rooms, yet for some reason, certain people go to the ER the second a drip of snot drops from their nose. On my most recent visit, a guy waiting for test results in the 'test results waiting area' came in for a mild rash. What lunatic goes to the emergency room for a mild rash? He should do what most men do – rub some cigarette ashes on that shit and go to bed. Cures 90 percent of our issues. Why anyone would subject themselves to a hospital trauma center on a Friday night because they got an itch is beyond my comprehension. Unless the rash was bleeding or literally on fire, you can wait a few days to see what happens. See what develops. Find out where the rash is taking you. Don't go the emergency room! Stay home, watch TV and drink some rubbing alcohol like a normal person.

Now that I have a family, I've been to the hospital more than I did in the first 38 years of my life. That's because

I had a son with my wife Rita. When Max was pushing to get out of the womb, our mutual friend Sandro called me at work (no tuna sandwich involved) and I sprinted from the office, into a cab, brought Rita downstairs, jumped into the cab, bolted into the hospital, got Rita to the maternity ward, then had a nurse look at her and tell us to come back tomorrow. Apparently, she wasn't ready, hardly dilated, and Max needed more time to cook. We came home where Rita sat on the couch writhing in pain. Somehow, I managed to get some sleep so I could prepare for what appeared to be a long and slow fight. Our friend Larissa and I eventually walked Rita to the hospital on a gorgeous, sunny Tuesday. Rita didn't appreciate the sunny day, the clear blue skies, the light breeze, or anything whatsoever because we made her walk to the hospital in terrible labor pain. She still hasn't forgiven me, but someone told us that's what we should do, *walk to the hospital*, so we did it. I'm not sure who that person was. Maybe gravity and some solid footsteps would shake Max loose.

This time they checked us in. Rita had a nice room. I stuck my head between her legs, but Max wasn't coming. The doctor stuck his head in there. A few nurses too. Then her OBGYN. Then the head of the hospital even snooped around her vagina. I believe the janitor eventually took a gander as well. I'm not sure what member of the hospital *didn't* take a look. But after "what seemed like a month," Rita had a C-section.

She recovered for five days, and Max for seven in the ICU. I would come back every day to check on them both. That was the most times I've ever been to a hospital on consecutive days. On the seventh day we took Max home and rested.

Years later, after going to the hospital to get Max ear tubes to reduce the amount of ear infections he was having, I went to the hospital to visit my buddy Mark when he got tossed into a mental institution. This was actually my second visit to a mental hospital, the first being my ex-girlfriend's neighbor who went missing one day. It's as nutty as you can imagine. Besides the creepy sterilized nature of the place, there's an incredible amount of apathy from the staff who assume most of its clientele are *cuckoo for Cocoa Puffs* and not worth paying attention to. They assume their brains are short-circuited, melting into porridge, or permanently switch to 'nuts' and beyond repair. If the patients picked up instruments, they could record an album with Captain Beefheart.

My wife got sick just a few years ago with some rare stomach virus that needed an incredibly dense antibiotic to treat. She had to choke down pills sized for a horse's mouth, which made her nauseous, but she got over it. Then my son got a stomach thing, then we returned about six months later because he got Salmonella. Somehow, we avoided the COVID-19 scourge.

What's most troubling is *I know* I'll be back at the hospital in some form or another. The percentages just tip that way. I'd prefer the reason be because *I'm* ill and not my family. The hospital is stressful enough, but watching the people you love suffer is maddening. Maybe I'll be admitted for something simple like getting knocked in the head with a beer bottle or overcome by a vicious foot fungus. These maladies can chew up my bad hospital juju, leaving the terrible maladies to somebody else.

Till Death

I remember the party taking place on the West side of Manhattan in a music club and bar. I went because my friend Susy invited me. She told me there'd be some free booze, and if I was calculated, I could stumble under a door key of cocaine in a bathroom stall. It was Monday, a slow night in most towns, even Manhattan. Certainly, a foreboding night for a party. Nothing was happening on stage where you'd normally find a raucous troupe of horns, or some guy in sunglasses choking a screaming guitar.

On the way, I ran into Susy and her friend Chloe emerging from the A train subway. Apparently, we were celebrating the engagement of their friends, who, I was told as we strolled along in the dark street, were not quite a stellar match. That was the only info I was privy to. "You'll see when you get there," was my only nugget. My mind ran wild. Was it two men… one 300 pounds and the other 100 pounds soaking wet with rocks in his pockets? A hetero couple where the woman was eight-feet tall the man four? A rhinoceros and a koala bear? Shotgun wedding? What was the matchup?

I was left to figure it out myself after a trail of bread-crumbs led me to the door. Kenny and Melissa were already partying like rocks stars – numbing themselves to the point of ridiculousness when we entered. The mouthwash of the evening was straight vodka. The cologne too. I would say they were ecstatic about the announcement, but this was more like a bad joke gone too far… a dare… no, a DOUBLE dare, and it wouldn't stop until everyone who doubted them had paid in full – or issued statements of impropriety by engraving apologies on their tombstones.

Kenny was as effeminate a man as I had ever met. I'd say he was flaming, but he may have been tamping it down for the ultimate performance of heterosexual nuptials. His every movement was more exaggerated than a Broadway star. After a joke, he'd tossed his head back in laugher until his Adams Apple nearly popped from his throat, and he rolled his eyes and collapsed at every bad story until he was limped over like a sleeping bag. His receding, wispy blond hair glowed under the lights as he glided back and forth between guests like an ice-dancer, occasionally catching his "fiancée" in a momentary embrace to laugh or twist each other around.

Melissa was not butch, but her plain, muscular face was socked under an orange helmet of tight, un-styled curls, which gave one the impression she gave up in the 4th grade. Her daily routine couldn't have constituted more than a quick brush-swipe across the teeth, a slap on the cheeks, and a smell-check of the armpits. She had the posture of an Olympic shot-put champ, and the personality of granite. Her loose jeans and oversized shirt said more than words ever could. And she was definitely along for the ride. Maybe in the driver's seat.

If I wasn't told about the situation beforehand, I'd have thought this was performance art – a bad act where tickets were given away for free. You didn't need a gaydar to know these two were homosexuals. The cliches were being spooned out like free mashed potatoes. For some reason, these two blind mice were tying the knot with each other *instead* of someone of their desired sex, which was their own.

I was assured by a few people (some who were no doubt on heavy drugs and slurping strong alcohol) that *no, this was not a marriage of convenience or for the purpose of a green card...* this was a marriage between two conscious, clear-minded adults who were "nuts" about each other. Nuts being the optimal term as these two were ready to be tossed into some kind of mental institution for crimes against human nature and destiny. Not only that, I was told in the bathroom while hunting for some blow that this was the *second* party these two love birds were throwing; the first taking place in Florida with family, where, no doubt, grandpa and Uncle Stew got to toss shit back into the faces of all the naysayers convinced they were both queer as three dollar bills, and would never, *ever* marry someone of the opposite sex.

As the night proceeded, the guests became more despondent -- *They were doing this.* They were *ACTUALLY* doing this. This wasn't the end, but it was the 11th hour. The final call before it went to legal papers and tumbling waterfalls of legal issues.

I caught Susy's face at one point, and she resembled someone gifted an extra-large bag of farts. Chloe too. I must have caught everyone at some point shaking their heads in dismay. Normally people who are drinking free cocktails and vacuuming rails of cocaine are more joyous than the crowd in attendance. *This* resembled a goodbye party for folks boarding a sinking ship. Like a group of people mentally preparing their "I told you so" speeches. After Kenny and Melissa asked everyone to join them to toast their "undying love" for the 38th time, people became unhinged. Usually when couples are smitten like kittens, it comes across in their body language. It doesn't need to be announced every 10 minutes like a train arrival. After we'd all tossed back sip number 39 on the night, it dredged up some deep feelings. Some people felt they needed to get mouthy -- to speak up or FINALLY say something.

There were some murmurs and perhaps some denials. Nothing over the top and not a full teardown or accusation. I saw someone claw at Kenny's arm and he pulled away dramatically, like a southern belle escaping to another room so she could pull herself together. I wasn't sure if this was a plea for Kenny to drink less or go suck a dick, which in this case would have been sage advice. After multiple trips to the bathroom, I came away with only an empty bladder and an emptier nose. Somehow, I'd missed the part of the party where the coke was being distributed freely.

Susy told me a few of the couple's closest confidants had already tossed out their fair share of appeals. The "are you sure?" and "have you thought this through?" pleas had been distributed to both parties completely. Not only on this night, but previously in other settings, both together and separately. The happy couple would have none of it.

As the shindig wound to a close, they must have sensed the storm rising again because they made a final declaration of their love and assured everyone that they were ecstatically happy and doing the "right thing" which is a strange announcement to make. Normally you shouldn't need to persuade your friends and family, as well as strangers who recoils in terror at the sight of your obvious sexual incompatibility, that you're doing the *right* thing. Me included. That sort of thing comes across in a vibe.

So, what became of this super happy couple? Well, believe it or not, they went through with the marriage and had two children... then, they both came out of the closet and lived a free and happy life as homosexuals, while co-parenting their children. Shocking, no?

Easy Come,
(not so) Easy Go

There we were, Kevin and I, tucked into a booth in a dark scotch and soda restaurant in South Carolina. Dim as a disco and lush with red leather and mahogany wood. Kevin said I had a gift for sniffing out good restaurants and he's right. I still do. It's not just aesthetics, but a certain vibe. Maybe I can do a quick count of the cars outside, or the quality of the signage, although, some of my favorite eateries have no signs and the best places in my town have lousy parking – if none at all. Maybe the people coming out the front door have unbuckled their pants, or I can pick up the scent of food from a distance, its quality determined before the place comes into view while cresting a hill.

We were stuffing our faces after 17 hours on the road and contemplating between mouthfuls of chicken cordon bleu if we had the fortitude to go all the way to New Orleans. Filled to the brim with southern cuisine and woozy from our late start, we decided to get a cheap motel and crash. Carrie, the friend of Kevin's sister who was hosting our stay, wasn't expecting us till the next day, and we were in no rush.

I checked us into a flea-bitten motel where the lanky proprietor asked who I was checking in with, and when I pointed to Kevin in the car, he smirked like a teenager catching us in a gay love affair. I suppose it was better than the alternative of being gunned down or lynched. Squeaking did emanate from our rusty, broken motel beds, but that's because we drank warm Pabst Blue Ribbon and cackled like idiots at some guy named Norm doing a "Wiener Dog" routine on TV.

The next day, we hit the road well before sunrise so we could be in southern Georgia, hunting down R.A. Miller, a folk/outsider artist whose work appeared in R.E.M. videos. Kevin was a big R.E.M. fan, so we swung by Miller's home and "studio," a tin shack that was rusting to the ground. When we arrived, R.A. was mowing his "lawn"– patches of dry dirt weaving through piles of rusting junk. With a red truckdriver ball cap pressed over his eyes and red suspenders slung over a dirty white T-Shirt, R.A. looked like someone you might find dying in a Steinbeck novel. We were greeted by his wife who walked us over to him. R.A. cut the mower engine and looked in our general direction, but not actually *at* us. I believe his eyesight was poor, but his brain had decades of hot Georgia heat baked into it. Kevin told him how much he liked his work, and R.A.'s response was nothing more than a grunt. It was not a stimulating conversation. We each bought art pieces for 10 bucks – Kevin a *Snake* and a *Blow Oscar* and me, two *Devils*… all of them cut from thick tin and painted with house paint. Something a fifth grader could do with more style and panache. We tried to shake his hand goodbye, but he just stared over our shoulders. Either he didn't shake hands on principle, or he didn't see us. I believe all he wanted to do in life was to continue to mow his dirt.

20 years later I sold my two *Devils* on eBay for $40.

Eventually we rolled into the Big Easy in midafternoon. We found ourselves driving the wrong way down a one-way street when a group of city kids playing wiffleball yelled, "stop!" After they hurled a bevy of insults in our face, they courteously gave us proper directions. Eventually, we parked my 1985 gold Honda Civic in front of Carrie's house – a well-kept shotgun cottage just off the Charles Street station line.

The door was locked, but Carrie told us to come to her work, a pizza place "nearby" where she'd give us the key so we could settle in. Because we didn't know the city too well, we walked to the pizza place through fields, back roads, shanty towns, and a whole array of landscapes that felt like two or three different cities rolled into one. It felt like an eternity, but when we eventually arrived, Carrie informed us we may have walked the most dangerous route possible through New Orleans. After that sobering tidbit, and a passable slice of pizza, Kevin and I took New Orleans by storm… our clueless path embedding a strange sense of fearlessness that we checked at the city limits. Any dive bar or two-bit po-boy shop that took our fancy, we two lanky, wide-eyed Yankees, desperate for a heaping dose of southern culture, patronized. My nose for cuisine got us stuffed with shrimp, Gumbo and enough Jazz music to fill a jukebox.

Tuesday night, we stomped to The Rebirth Brass Band at the Maple Leaf and drank like fish until we stumbled to a diner around the corner for breakfast, another satisfying spot I sniffed out that we were later told was one of the best in the city. We drank beers under sagging strands of lights in outdoor bars that were no different than someone's backyard, then watched a guy shred a guitar in a living reincarnation of Jimi Hendrix on Bourbon Street. We combed through the catacombs of an old bookstore in the French Quarter where Kevin paid 10 bucks for the hand-written diary of a 16-year-old Kentucky girl that was crammed with enough sweet memories to warm the heart, and enough erotica to shock a sailor on shore leave. Kev and I took turns flipping through and reading passages to each other... her 14th birthday party, the death of her dog, and when she fucked her boyfriend in the flatbed of his pickup truck under the starry skies, tag-teamed by his buddy and another friend who she didn't know too well, but because he brought a bottle of vodka... well, you know, he seemed like he deserved to get laid for his efforts.

Carrie's house was sparsely furnished, with nothing more than a couch and coffee table, and an empty dining room where Kevin and I crashed in sleeping bags on the hard wood floor. After two days, she got two more visitors – a chic, smarmy, yet charming Italian named Marco, who donned a thin goatee and slicked-back hair, and his petite blond American girlfriend Tess, who was super uptight and acted as if she was in the wrong place at the wrong time *all the time*. They had just flown in from Italy and wanted to take in the town.

"If you liked The Rebirth Brass Band at the Maple Leaf, go to Spencer's," suggested Carrie, "you'll love it. You'll probably be the only white people there, but it's the best place to see a show."

That challenge was accepted. Kevin and I, along with

Marco and Tess, danced the night away at Spencer's. Sure enough, we were the only white people there. They couldn't have been nicer. We did dance-offs in the middle of clapping pits of people who whooped and hollered like you read about. Even Tess, who hadn't shed her cold exterior the entire time, began to melt to the music.

Between sets, we shared joint with an old man hanging outside the window of his apartment's street-level living room.

"It's so cool that you white folks came to this neighborhood. We need more people like you over here," he said puffing on the giant joint I rolled, through his thick, white mustache.

The next day, a warm and sunny Friday hanging with humidity, Kev and I dug through various record shops and found a coveted copy of Funkadelic's *One Nation Under A Groove*, complete with bonus 45 containing four extra songs. The album hadn't been released on CD, and we were desperate to listen to it. We took our newfound treasure, along with our memories and prepared to hit the road back to New York.

That night, as a final send-off, Carrie took us to see Boozoo Chavis, the famous Zydeco musician. We arrived at a bowling alley around 7:00pm, which I figured was a bowling alley converted into a music venue, but nope, it was just a bowling alley. A very nice bowling alley. High end and sophisticated. Upon entering, we were met with pins crashing around the hard wood lanes and people packed in tight. We stood nipping bottles of beer, chatting with the locals, and milled about.

Within minutes, everyone stopped bowling, a spotlight hit the wall, musicians hit a small stage and Zydeco music blasted throughout the place. Boozoo Chavis howled into a mic, and everyone hit the dance floor – like a flash mob. Kevin and I stood dumbfounded as every single person in the place jumped in. Black teens, white old ladies, fat guys and thin girls, big and small, short and tall – all cutting a rug. They were swinging, two-stepping, line dancing, do-se-doing, hooking arms and tossing each other around like rag dolls. It was nuts. Kevin and I could hardly make sense of it. New Yorkers move fast, but the big easy can move pretty quick too. We stood in awe at the complete synchronicity of the event. Eventually, we jumped into the action, joining in on some kind of electric slide that involved clapping and bowing like cowpoke introductions at the hoe-down. Two goofy New Yorkers moving like giraffes to the music.

But that wasn't it. Apparently, this was a showdown between Boozoo Chavis and Buckwheat Zydeco, two of the premiere Zydeco artists in the world. I mean, Buckwheat Zydeco has *Zydeco* in his name! They went at it, squeezing their accordions, clacking their washboards, stomping to the beat, and driving every Zydeco fan wild. It was a long night of dancing and drinking.

We woke early the next day hungover, tired, foggy and buzzed from the fun. But, it was time to hit the road.

As we tossed our junk into the trunk of the car, a snowflake fell before our eyes. Carrie, being a smart and caring friend, leaned her forearm against the driver's side window and suggested we stay in New Orleans for a few more days.

"It hasn't snowed in New Orleans in something like 50 years. The weather's not supposed to be too good. Maybe stick around till it passes."

For some reason, we shrugged her off. Not only did we school in Syracuse, a place that snowed daily nine months out of the year, but I was an expert driver in the snow and my little Honda, equipped with front wheel drive, was great on slick streets.

"*You* may be good in the snow, but the south is not. We don't get snow down here."

Once again, we shrugged her off. Maybe drinking heavily and sleeping on hard maple for five days hardened our heads, or perhaps we were simply stupid, but the thought of making a Cannonball Run from New Orleans to Upstate New York before the country shut down seemed too juicy a challenge to pass up. There was a huge winter storm passing through the United States from Mexico to North Dakota and it was quickly moving east. If we took the right path, gunned the car at blazing speeds, and didn't get lost, we could get to Syracuse before the snow fell *really* hard.

We zoomed out of town, as confident and upbeat as we were naive. By the time we got to Baton Rouge, snow-flakes dusted the windshield like any snowstorm in any northern city. We had the opportunity to turn around, but we crossed over a small bridge, and that alone felt like a sign from the Gods to keeping moving. Besides, it was still partly sunny, and we were buzzed – full of food, last evenings booze, and flowing with the irrational confidence.

We drove on... straight into the great unknown.

It was a terrible, *terrible* mistake.

•••

Even though we took Route 95 and Route 20 down most of the way, we decided, for some unknown reason, to take 59 to 81 back up, which would take us through Mississippi, Alabama and Tennessee – three states that rank low on the education system, but rank high on the gun and banjo ownership hierarchy.

By the time we got to Birmingham, Alabama, we knew we were in deep, deep trouble. Carrie had been completely correct. The south was (and still is to this day) not prepared for *any* type of snowy weather. A mere 4 hours into our trip, the roads were littered with cars that had jack-knifed off the sides like nuclear war had ravaged the lands. There were cars facing backward, cars that had bee-lined into the woods, cars plopped vertically in ditches with front-ends up in the air, and cars completely upside down with their hazard lights flashing. It was utterly stupefying. Making the scene more ridiculous was the fact that there was only about a quarter of an inch of snow on the ground… blacktop road still visible under the wispy white coating.

The only saving grace for us were the roads being free of cars, so we towed behind a row of competent drivers, mostly from northern states.

Of the many mistakes we made on our trip other than getting into the car in the first place, was refusing to check a weather station or newscast to see what we were getting into. The storm, one of the biggest to hit the United States in its history, had come much faster than anticipated. The roads continued to get worse, and by the time we got to the outskirts of

Chattanooga Tennessee, we were forced to drive in one lane behind rows of slow-moving cars as the roads had formed a sort of frozen rail track channel; something an amusement park ride may take you through.

We stopped into a massive truck-stop hub, a place with an absurd amount of gas pumps, plus a grocery store and BBQ diner/restaurant. The place was *jammed* with people – a safe haven from the madness of the storm. Again, it felt like the apocalypse – a contingency of the lost and broken who funneled in from the mayhem.

Kev and I parked and headed into the buzz of manic diner activity. It reminded me of a ski lodge at lunch – patrons packed like sardines in thick clothes, half wet, with bed-head and rosy cheeks. Every table was stuffed with people, scraping lunch forks over plates and blathering about the coming weather and what to do about it. A beefy, sandy-haired truck driver in a red checkered flannel jacket, slugged a mouthful of coffee and stated with emphatic wisdom that he wasn't "taking my rig out there again. I'll be stuck out there for days." If experienced truckers were shutting down for the storm; why shouldn't we?

The diner walls were strewn with televisions, all fixed on weather channels with concerned looking newscasters analyzing the grim details on maps. Kevin and I grabbed food at the takeout counter and surveyed the room. Wandering wide-eyed and open-eared, we took in bits of conversation while nipping on coffee. Some people were heading out, others staying put. I caught a short, dark-haired trucker tell his tablemate that, "they" were going to shut down the main roads. I leaned in and asked if "they" were going to shut down *all* the roads.

"I don't think they can. That's too many roads to shut down. The smaller roads will be open, but they won't be drivable."

Kev and I took in our surroundings and contemplated a decision; sit inside a Tennessee truck stop for two days, or head out with a small band of adventurers into the great and snowy unknown? Considering there wasn't a seat to be had, and we were always up for an adventure, we hit the road.

Back on the icy rail track, we crept through the back roads, which weren't so hard to navigate, but crept along at a frustrating 20 miles per hour. As the day turned into a grey evening, we'd been on the road for nearly 10 hours and hadn't yet reached the halfway mark of Tennessee. During that time, the storm was blowing through, and the road condition were about as bad as they could be. Devastating winds and white-out conditions. The windshield wipers carved a white viewing port that narrowed by the second.

Kevin, working an ancient map, navigated us as the darkness of the back country made the driving a harrowing experience. I don't remember eating, going to the bathroom or getting out of the car for the next chunk of time. It seemed we were doggedly determined to get home, leaning forward in our seats like it would propel our momentum with dynamic force. As the conditions became worse and the back roads smaller and slipperier, it became increasingly clear that we were alone. The train of cars that we'd hitched to for hours had all but disappeared – our little golden Honda tooling around tiny roads in an unknown state.

Eventually we found a small deli and stopped for supplies, relieved ourselves and recalculated our bearings.

A quick overview of the television indicated the storm had passed the south already, but was still lingering in the northeast. So, Kevin and I made the first wise decision of our trip. We decided to go west, *then* go north, following behind the storm. Our reasoning being that by the time we got to the northern states who had snow equipment, the plows would have cleared the way in the hours before we arrived at a particular destination.

By the time we ventured out of Kentucky, the roads began to open up a bit. Our gamble was paying off. We'd take Route 70 through Ohio, up to Route 90, which ran along Lake Erie and back-end through Buffalo, New York, until we reached Syracuse University. A solid six- or seven-hour drive under normal, clear conditions.

At that point, it was midnight and I'd been behind the wheel for 15 hours. Kevin took over the driving and I navigated the map. It was another in a long line of bad decisions. Cruising through a small back road, Kevin, originally from Los Angeles and not conditioned to driving in snow, lost control of the wheel and drove us right into a four-foot snow embankment. Foom! The snow blanketed over the top of the car like a quilt, and all I saw was a wall of white. Kevin opened the door and climbed out, the Honda glowing inside the igloo as The Ink Spots *I Don't Want to Set the World on Fire* lullabied on the stereo.

I was despondent. But what could I do? I was exhausted and not fit to argue or get mad. I figured the igloo was as good a place as any to rest for the night, as long as a snowplow didn't crush us while we slept, or we didn't suffocate or freeze to death. Some 12 hours before, we were passing by the array of terrible drivers who jack-knifed off the side of the road like slaughtered cattle. Now *we* were the cattle, stuck in a pit of despair.

Kevin mentioned having Triple A car coverage and if we could get to a phone, we could call a tow truck. We were in the middle of nowhere country, not a street- or house-light in sight. How we'd get to a phone I didn't know, but after 20 minutes, a set of headlights glimmered in the distance, and an old man in a pick-up truck pulled over and asked if we needed help. After some back and forth, Kevin hopped in the truck and went to either phone AAA, or disappear, never to be seen alive again.

Sitting inside the igloo, my mind ran wild as to what could possibly happen to him. *Silence of the Lambs* was still fresh in our minds, and after 15 minutes, I assumed the kindly old man had Kevin strung up on a hook and was lopping fresh steaks out of his midsection to feed his inbred family of ax murderers. To my surprise and relief, Kevin was back in about 30 minutes – safe and sound with all his limbs. It was a looooong 30 minutes.

"Tow truck will be here in an hour." Kevin said.

When 2:00 am clicked on the clock, two high beams cut through the clear, dark night, and a tow truck arrived. A large, bearded man in overalls hopped out, and within seconds, he had the little Honda yanked from the frozen rabbit hole. The tow man wiped his hands with a rag and waved goodbye. The Honda fired up and off we went. This time, with me back at the wheel.

"I don't think I should drive again," Kevin admitted sheepishly.

It didn't matter. Navigating a series of flat back roads, we entered northern Ohio and somewhere outside of Cleveland, the engine popped, and a guizer of steam shot up from the hood – the radiator bubbled over. Once again, we found ourselves stuck on the side of the road. We threw up our hands and figured, like we had hours before, *this* was as good a place as any to bunk down for the night. Standing on the desolate road in the cold, dark night, looking at the empty void, we once again saw two headlights appear in the distance until a small, red, beat-up two-door Honda pulled up next to us and rolled down the window. It was a guy our age, high as a kite – two beaming red eyes, and two braided pig tails shooting straight out from the sides of his head like handlebars on a bicycle.

"You guys need help?" He asked.

"Car overheated," I said, "you have any water?"

"Sure," he said, and produced a large red thermos of water, enough to fill up the radiator and cool it down.

Listening to our adventure, he offered his apartment floor to crash on, but we told him since we'd come *this* far, we might as well go all the way. He understood and waved goodbye as we got onto Route 90.

After a grueling, endless drive along Lake Erie from Cleveland to Buffalo, where the snow went from deep, to towering mountains of white, we came to an embankment of toll booths as the night sky began to brighten with the dawn of a new day. Confronted with a mass of yellow flashing lights from heavy plow trucks and barriers of flickering road signs, we were informed, via giant black lettering, that Route I-90 E had been shut down until further notice. After all the backroads and setbacks, both real and imagined, we'd finally come to the ultimate wall. That was it… end of the line. There was no real way to get through as the backroads were undrivable at that point. Besides getting its *usual* snow during a snowstorm, Northern New York gets "lake effect snow" which is moisture that comes off Lake Erie and freezes in the air, adding inches, and in this case FEET of snow to an already devastating total.

I turned the Honda around, went to a small village, and zipped into parking spot in front of a shopping strip – the glow of a laundromat's neon lights illuminating the towers of snow embankments, and our final failure. I shut the engine, cranked the seat back, folded my arms and closed my eyes. Kevin did the same.

We tried to sleep, or pretend to sleep, but at that point, the adrenaline and lack of rest had worked a wacky overtired buzz in our souls that wouldn't let us rest.

"I can't sleep," I admitted.

"Let's just go." Kevin said. "Get on the highway. We're almost there."

"Let's do it." I concurred.

I fired up the Honda, backed out of the spot, and had the car confronting the toll booth embankment like a tugboat against an armada. It was still dark enough to slip through the booths unnoticed, and no one seemed to be manning the area as the crews had retired for the night. I found a hole and got on 90 towards Syracuse and didn't look back. Free (monetarily) and clear (from the law).

The city of Buffalo was still glowing with lights as we passed, a veritable winter wonderland. Route 90 was completely empty, not a car in sight, and the Honda rumbled and clacked over the frozen road as the dawn turned into a stunningly clear blue day.

We finally entered Syracuse, got off the highway and climbed up one of its many hilly roads towards the University. If the Tennessee truck stop was the epitome of buzzing madness, Syracuse was the complete opposite – an utter ghost town. Not one person, not one car. The city got well over four feet of snow, and by the time the roads had been cleared, the plows had formed walls eight feet high. Like a child's toy in a world of white Lego brick barricades, the Honda tooled through the maze as I tried to landmark the area by building roof tops and muscle memory.

As the 11 O'clock sun gleamed off the towering walls of snow, Kevin shifted uneasily, grabbing the edge of the seat as the car fishtailed and bounced.

"Oh, boy." He said uneasily.

I could hear it in his voice.

"You okay?" I asked.

"I need the bathroom… now!"

As the Honda slipped and slid to the top of the hill, I fought the wheel and tapped the break like the foot pedal of my drum kit, the Honda handling like a clumsy Zamboni.

"Oh man, hurry!"

Kevin immediately reached DEFCON 1. We hardly used the bathroom during the maddening trip, and the body knows when you're almost home and unconsciously releases the intestinal muscles, dropping all waste into the colon for near immediate evacuation. Every turn on every slick street corner felt like an eternity, as I bent the fishtailing Honda around. By the time we were a few corners away, Kevin's anxiety turned to outright panic.

"I'm going to shit myself!"

I skidded the Honda in front of our house, the two-story box incased in a monumental block of snow. There was no path, no driveway clearance. Nothing but a crisp slab of frozen water no less than eight feet high fenced across our home. Gangly Kevin, all six-foot-two of him, hurtled the wall like an Olympic long jumper, blasting through with a powdery explosion, and deep into the pliable powder. I saw nothing but the top of his dark head as it bounced up and down in the ice cream cake, until his body resurfaced at the top of our front steps where he fought through snow drifts until he hammered into the front door like a football running back.

I simply left the car where I stopped. There were no parking spots. Nothing but an endless maze of white walls. I followed Kevin's trail into the house where he greeted me with a crooked smile.

"Didn't think I was going to make it."

We plopped down on the couch and breathed a long sigh of relief.

27 hours after we left New Orleans, we arrived safely in Syracuse with not a whole lot to show for it. The weather stranded the entire student body at their spring break destinations for two more days. Any need to rush back was rendered null and void. Why we felt compelled to return to Syracuse was unclear. A mission I suppose. An idiotic test of endurance… or stupidity. Instead of sitting comfortably in New Orleans, drinking beer and listening to Jazz and Zydeco, we sat in our abandoned Syracuse ice castle doing nothing. Leaving the Big Easy wasn't a smart idea, but leaving that Tennessee

gas/diner hub was. Like Syracuse, that section of Tennessee *also* got four feet of snow, and although they do get snow in Tennessee, not four feet. It turned out to be the 1993 *Storm of the Century*. Even the Florida panhandle got about 12 inches of snow, and New Orleans about three.

Kevin eventually went over to his girlfriend's house, and I went over to my buddy Tim's to smoke bong hits all day. Later, the four of us met at Chuck's Tavern and drank until everyone filtered back into town to finish the Spring semester.

My little gold Honda, who persevered through thick and thin, sat naked on the side of the road for days, making it an easy target for the city's meter maids. For some unknown reason, I got a parking ticket for $45. When I called the City of Syracuse to inquire as to where they thought was a proper place to park after a once-in-a-generation snowstorm, they said, "good point" and tore the ticket up.

Taste Menu

We spend a lot of time manipulating food to make it palatable. I, for one, don't really like goat cheese. It has the consistency of yogurt mixed with sawdust. Like licking a chalkboard. My sister laid some goat cheese out one Christmas that was mixed with chives and it was the most delicious thing I ever ate. I was spreading it on crackers and popping it in my mouth like a pill addict. Like someone tossing popcorn down their throat at the movies. I guess chives did the trick. Same goes for Avocados. To me they taste like thick lettuce, but whip it up with onions and lime and some other shit, scoop it with corn chips, and before you know it, you can't eat the enchiladas you ordered for your main course.

When Marco Polo invented spices (or something like that) he invented recipes. I'm not a historian. Don't give that as an answer if it comes up on *Trivial Pursuit*. Marco Polo definitely invented that swimming pool game where people shout his name with their eyes closed. Not water polo. That's when you swim with horses and play soccer. I missed the last Olympics, and I believe that's how it's played. Regular Polo, a game with horses on land, is a game he didn't invent even though his name is part of it. That's golf on horses. I don't know who invented the land Polo game, but it seems pretty nuts. Horses are insanely muscular creatures who will toss you onto the ground like a rag doll if they choose. All they eat is hay, which is sad if you think about it.

Spices, herbs, fruit and seasonings go a long way to make food taste tastier. Have you ever eaten a chicken breast without seasoning? It's torture. Might as well eat a throw pillow. It gives you the same satisfaction as eating a snowball. Zero. Toss the chicken breast in a skillet with honey and lemon and rosemary and you've got something happening. That's what chefs do. They invent flavor combinations for food, so you can go out and have something to eat because you have no imagination and you're too lazy to cook. Some chefs go a little overboard with the cooking. They'll serve a bird head on a plate with rainbow chutney and a dollop of emotions. You'll pay $300 but need to eat a food-cart pretzel or go to bed with tears in your eyes.

I decided recently that I don't like apples. They do nothing for me. They actually give me a headache. I saw a guy on the news who has preserved over 150 varieties of apples. That guy will never be my friend. I love oranges. Can he rediscover some lost orange varieties? Apples have very distinctive looks, but all oranges look the same. Ever bought oranges and realized you bought Cara Cara oranges? Those are red inside. Not blood oranges. Those are the oranges they dig up in Africa. People die for those things. It's sad, really.

They're just oranges. They grow on trees here. But maybe not in Africa. They smuggle them in and pay big money – sell them to gangsters. They're excellent with breakfast.

My wife makes orange chicken. Not like the Chinese food style, but her own way. She's Brazilian. She tosses chicken in a skillet and squeezes an orange over it. That's it. She's not Marco Polo or anything, but she can cook well enough. She just invented orange chicken one day. I think there's onions in it too. Maybe salt. She's very light on the salt. She has high blood pressure, so she keeps the salt very low. We have that pink salt which is from the Himalayas. I believe that's where people climb to the top and some of them die while climbing. They freeze like frozen chicken. The sherpas just leave them where they fall and use them as trail markers. Pretty grim. I don't like mountain climbing. Too much work. I sit at home and eat. The pink salt grinder claims it's salt that's been unearthed after a thousand years, yet the container has an expiration date. Perhaps if they used the salt on the frozen climbers, they'd defrost so they can be tossed down the mountain.

Worse than plain chicken is plain turkey. My neighbor's fence has more taste. Less dry too. That'd why the pilgrims invented gravy. Don't quote me on that. I'm not a history teacher. Marco Polo wasn't involved. I think Christopher Columbus invented gravy. Double check that before you take a test or anything. He came on the Mayflower and showed the Indians how to drizzle it on turkey. He thought America was India, so he called the locals Indians. They're Native Americans. I'm sure the Native Americans had a better name for America than America, but I don't know what it is. Christopher Columbus also directed that *Home Alone* movie where the kid sets traps for those bumbling burglars. How he managed to invent gravy and direct a blockbuster film is beyond my comprehension. I think the Native Americans set traps for Columbus, but it didn't work. So, the film is not factual at all.

I'm not a fan of Cauliflower. I like Broccoli, but cauliflower sucks. It tastes like a tub of piss someone farted in. Still, my wife makes me eat it. She roasts it with herbs or flavor or something. I'm not a food critic. My palette isn't that sophisticated. They make cauliflower pizza dough. It's not as bad as it sounds. It's worse. Eat a car bumper or something more enjoyable. People say broccoli and cauliflower taste the same, but that's bullshit. Broccoli tastes good and cauliflower tastes like death. The people who make James Bond films claim they invented broccoli. I believe them. James Bond is a lot like the kid in the Home Alone movies except instead of stopping burglars, he's thwarting megalomaniacs with nuclear bombs. Both use clever traps and household materials as weapons.

I'm not a huge fan of popcorn either. Not that popcorn has a fan club. Maybe it does. I'm not a member. How would one join? Only assholes dislike popcorn, but I swear, I'm not an asshole. A pain in the ass, but not an asshole. Popcorn's ratio of scratchy, choking bits to actual enjoyable popped corn is way too high for me. You can be munching handfuls of buttery corn at the movies, then suddenly you're hacking up a fistful of thumbtacks. I've eaten buckets of popcorn and endured at least one full-blown choke-fest with each bucket. Probably during a Christoper Columbus hit film. I think he did one about Marco Polo.

I don't like corn either. I don't know why it's popular. You can purchase 10 ears for a dollar. They practically give it away. "Here, eat this corn or we'll feed it to the hogs." Hogs will eat their own shit. We're basically one level removed from pigs. I've heard humans taste similar to pigs. I wouldn't know. I haven't eaten humans… that I know of. Someone could have slipped me a thigh or an elbow when I wasn't looking. How would I know? Scary to think about. Food is a mystery. The Native Americans ate people. Don't quote me on that. I'm not an anthropologist. They definitely ate corn. A lot of corn. They ground it in a maize. Why they felt it needed to be mashed into a giant puzzle is beyond me. People drown corn in butter. Same with popcorn. Is corn inedible without butter? And salt? I used to frequent a Cuban place that roasted the corn with spices. It made it better apparently. People lined up down the street for it. Cubans ate all the Native Americans. Don't take that as 100% fact. I didn't do well in school.

Strawberries are terrible unless they're in other foods. Like ice cream. Eat a raw strawberry and you end up grinding the little seeds in your teeth for days. Each strawberry comes with about 150 seeds. They flavor medicine with cherries. Kids love it but I quit drinking it years ago. My son drinks beverages with blue raspberry as a flavoring. It's not a real fruit. Raspberries come in a bunch of colors but blue isn't one of them. Why are these flavoring companies playing games? We had a friend who was allergic to blue. He consumed nothing blue. Even when he was sad. He grew out of it. Now he can eat blue all he wants, but he's not interested in blue. Even blueberries, which are tasty, and a natural blue. Who invented color? It's a fascinating business. And fruit? Who invented that? People eat it like it's growing on trees.

Food manipulation is big business. There are people mashing things together all the time. I once made mashed potatoes with mashed bananas. That was stupid. Tasted like defeat and sour socks. No amount of salt could save it. I'm not a chef. Everyone politely choked it down, but they swore to never come for dinner again. Happy accidents are the key to inventing new flavors. Chefs pile different foods on a kitchen table, put a bomb underneath and set it to blow. What lands on the floor afterwards is tasted and placed on a menu. At least that's how it works in my dreams. I'm sure it's more complicated than that. Sounds like the plot of a James Bond movie. Crazy chef threatens the world food supply. What's the title? No Time To Fry? Russian Dressing with Love? For Chicken Thighs Only? Sounds like a recipe for success.

My wife doesn't like lamb. Too gamey for her. My father likes mint jelly on lamb. Who invented that? Was a guy brushing his teeth and thought mint and jelly would be a wonderful combination? Probably some English knight invented mint jelly in the 1300's during the Black Plague. He probably invented mint chocolate chip ice cream too. That's why Columbus got the hell out of there and went with Marco Polo to India. Or something like that. I'm not a map maker or anything. My sister served fig jelly at Thanksgiving that we put on brie cheese with crackers and that was awesome. I tossed that back like it was oxygen. If it wasn't for my sister, I'd be eating Ritz Crackers and peanut butter for H'or Douerves. George Washington Carver invented peanuts. God bless him. I love peanut butter. He and George Washington along with Abraham Lincoln ate PB & Js during the Spanish American

War. Again, my timelines may be off a bit here. I'm not a historian.

People are into ancient grains these days. Quinoa and farrow. Talk about tough. A barrel of lawn clippings goes down easier. It's horse food. One must really add lots of herbs and spices to get that stuff down. Garlic, onions and a quart of 10W-30 motor oil. These were the foods of Jesus. Not motor oil, but farrow. Mia Farrow had nothing to do with it. Nor her son Ronan Farrow. The Farrows and Jesus never met. I don't know if the Farrows like farrow, but I would guess they love it. They may love Jesus, but that's a personal thing. I believe Ronan is Jewish. Or half Jewish. Jesus was a Jew, so they have that in common. I'm not a theologist. Don't quote me on these things.

Let's review. Columbus and Marco Polo were water game designers who traveled around the world inventing recipes. Along with Jesus, they managed to create recipes that we use today. Things like peanut butter and mint jelly. Our founding fathers were instrumental in getting films made about English spies and knights, all of them directed and produced by people who hate cauliflower – but were also chefs.

Don't take my word for it though. You should probably research some of this stuff yourself. I'm not a museum curator or anything.

Educational Films....
and You

In high school I took a driver's education class. It was generally worthless. We used car simulators in the dank basement of the school. With steering wheels stuck to fake 1960 dashboards, we "drove" in front of a screen that projected washed-out southern California streets. They were no more realistic than the roads they project behind the actors driving in the movies of the 1950s. Movies where characters muttered snappy dialogue as the road behind them swerved around knotty, cliff-hugging roads while the person driving in an obvious well-lit studio, barely turned the wheel. Your ability to suspend your disbelief hinged on those characters making it seem like they were *actually* driving a car on a real road, but the footage looked washed out and more outdated than the outdated people in the outdated car. You could almost hear the stagehands coughing up their lungs because of the hanging cigarette smoke.

I remember there was a narrator for these Driver's

Ed films. Some brush-cut guy with a grey suit living in a grey world. He stepped into frame and yammered about safety rules, all of which were ignored the second we got our grubby little hands on the steering wheel of our parent's cars. The only piece of advice I remember stated in the film was to: "aim high while driving." It's a good tip. I said that to my wife constantly when I was teaching her to drive because she always looked at the curb and came dangerously close to scraping the wheels against it, sending us careening to our deaths.

My wife grew up poor and didn't drive a car until she was about 40. She never had the pleasure of watching antiquated black and white Driver's Ed films where grandfatherly stiffs gave driving instructions while a Point-Of-View car camera drove through Los Angeles, passing '62 Plymouths and milk truck paddy wagons.

My Driver's Ed teacher was a short, balding guy with thick glasses and a large gap between his two front teeth named Mr. Marzone. The only thing I ever remember him telling us in class was a joke...

A man pulls over to fix the flat tire on his car. He stops in front of an insane asylum. He takes off the flat and changes it with the new tire, but realizes he can't find the four lug nuts he removed to replace the tire. He looks around and asks the crazy man behind the iron bars of the insane asylum if he took them.

"How could I have taken them, I'm behind bars here."
"That's true" the man says.
The crazy man then says: "why don't you take one lug nut from the remaining tires and put them on that tire. Then

you'll have three lugs for each tire and can drive to a repair shop."

The car owner says: "Hey, that's a great idea. You're pretty smart. You should be out here in the real world."

The crazy guys says: "Go out there? I may be crazy, but I'm not stupid!"

Mr. Marzone preceded to cackle like a villain from a James Bond movie after hitting the countdown button on a doomsday device. I looked over at my buddy Joel, and we gave each other the most perplexing look we could give one another.

It took the better part of 30 years, but I finally understand the joke, because, well… life. It doesn't make it funny… I mean, not *haha* funny, but I get the "joke."

I'm from the era where many of the school films we watched were reel-to-reel films projected onto filthy screens. It was the 1980s, but the films were all from the 1950s and 60s. Not only outdated, but of a certain quality one can only describe as in a state of "decrepitude." Occasionally, someone would wheel in a TV and VCR – the tape was popped in and our brains would turn off. The subject inconsequential. But, the VCR contained something in actual color and not a wash of muted greens and greys. The celluloid films were mind-numbing takes on subjects like protein, how ore is made into usable metal, or the history of the elemental table. Things that would put you to sleep instantly if you were at home or in an actual theater, but in the dreaded belly of high school, was like mainlining pure cocaine. Anything better than listening to the incessant drone of our teacher and their tedious lessons.

The films had punchy titles like *Everything is Protein!* and *Our Mr. Sun!* Titles that shook you from your slumber and made you beg the screen to answer the question "How *does* carbon affect me?" Questions no one asked until scientists started poking around the earth and digging up hunks of metal by the truckloads.

The films tended to be generally pleasant. Educational films don't make the rounds for over 30 years without having some staying power. The deep-voiced narrators and the catchy pizzicato music could lull any viewer into a zombie-like state. Especially high school students. Your teacher had a break for the day to let the film do the work so they could sit in the corner and grade the endless test papers that piled to the ceiling because they actually want a life at home.

I was the kid who usually ran the film projector. Not because I was an AV nerd, but because I loved film and I enjoyed being in the back – behind the camera. Once back there, no one could see me because the lens washed the room under a veil of light. Behind the veil, I could wander around, kick my feet up, or even lay on a table. Especially in spacious science classrooms where large examination tables could hold at least two or three people.

One of the more memorable films we watched in science class was an experiment conducted by an Austrian "scientist" named Theodore Erismann and his "research assistant" Ivo Kohler. Erismann forced his assistant Kohler, I assume at gunpoint, to wear these inversion goggles that made his vision flip upside down. They conducted exercises with Ivo's inverted view, like: poking each other with sticks, handling everyday items, and writing on paper. Eventually Kohler's mind readjusted his vision and flipped it correctly while wearing the glasses. He rode his bike down the street and even talked to people on the sidewalk. Once his goggles were removed, his vision was flipped upside down again, forcing Kohler to live life with an inverted brain. This affliction, according to our teacher Mr. Dennis, may have driven Kohler a little "cuckoo" as one might say in the field of psychology. This bit of news spurred a slew of questions from the class completely unrelated to the film itself.

"Was the assistant wrapped in a strait jacket?"

"Did they toss him in the looney bin?"

"Did he go completely insane, or did he eventually get better?"

"How many days was his vision fucked up?"

According to my teacher, Kohler's vision took a few weeks to flip back to normal. I can only assume that Kohler himself thought his brain would never readjust and went temporarily mad from the thought of it. What this film taught us I couldn't say. The only thing I gleaned from the lesson was to never fuck with your brain using optical equipment. That should be done with heavy doses of drugs.

Even though the laughably over-the-top educational "documentary" *Reefer Madness* was kicked to the curb while my parents were in kindergarten, it didn't top the industry from churning out films to warn the world's youth about the dangers of drugs and alcohol. *Sarah T. – Portrait of an Alcoholic*, was a classic about a girl named Sarah, hence the title, who's struggling with her parent's divorce, and school, and her sister, who's WAY better than her, and sweeping it into the dustbin under the powerful allure of alcohol. It stars America's favorite devil-possessed girl Linda Blair, as well as everyone's *second* favorite Jedi, Mark Hamill, the first favorite Jedi being Darth Vader of course.

Eventually, all the drugs were represented for our viewing pleasure… acid, marijuana and cocaine.

Many of the tough subjects were covered at home too. Not from our parents. Oh no… our parents were too busy getting high as hell to hand these lessons down. These lessons came in the form of "after school specials." They represented some of the more emotional, hardcore subjects. I remember a commercial for the special *Best Little Girl in the World* about a girl who was anorexic. I was traumatized just watching the advertisement. A father is brutally buttering a piece of bread while his hallowed-eyed daughter says, "I'm not gonna eat that!" The father counters through gritted teeth, "Oh, yes you are!" Then plugs the thick dry bread into her mouth. I'm not sure if you've studied medicine or not, but this isn't the cure for anorexia. The specials ranged from kids coping with having mentally disabled siblings, to kids dealing with parents with disabilities.

Then there's the Ben Affleck classic about a kid who throws his life away trying to get the competitive advantage in high school sports through steroids. I actually caught this in college, sitting on the couch after a class, immediately following a massive bong hit. I assumed the guy playing the lead would never amount to anything, and like many of my predictions, was completely wrong. At that point in time, these educational films were bordering on art. Anguish and good acting took over for cheesy narration and antiquated scolding.

Color film didn't hurt either.

I can only remember snippets of stuff like the upside-down vision film, and a movie we watched in class called *On Borrowed Time* about a man who manages to get Death caught in a tree. If I remember correctly, the family tricks him because Death has come to take the grandfather or something. I'm not sure. I didn't pay attention to that movie either. And that was shown in class for pure entertainment. Maybe in English class. Another black and white film from the archives of ancient history. I remember watching *The Lord of the Flies* (instead of reading the book I guess) and *The Sound of Music*. None of these things were educational besides getting graded papers returned to us quicker, and learning the *Do-Ray-Me* song.

One of my all-time favorites, seared into my memory, was a black and white film called *Full House* featuring five short stories by O. Henry. My favorite vignette featured a bum who keeps attempting to get tossed in jail by committing petty crimes to secure himself shelter for the coming winter. He does terrible things such as: steal an umbrella, and eats a large meal then refuses to pay, but there's always a reason he never gets hauled in… random distractions, sympathetic victims, etc. Finally, while talking to a fellow bum outside a church, he has an epiphany and decides he's going to turn his life around, only to be arrested for loitering and trespassing. It's what the kids today call *irony*. It starred Charles Laughton and Marilyn Monroe. I believe these films were the precursor to Audio Books. The only O. Henry story I remember reading in class was *The Gift of the Magi*. Everything else was projected onto a screen.

Working in advertising, my team and I face the conundrum of doing anti-drug campaigns that are not only effective, but won't be mocked by the youth, turning our messages into memes or catchphrases that do the opposite of what they were intended. These campaigns are exhausting and by the time we hammer out the message, massage the copy, obtain effective photography, video and design, while presenting supporting data about the dangers of drugs, we're ready to go to the nearest bar and get stupid, cock-eyed drunk.

I'm not sure if anyone really paid attention to these films, or were swayed by their powerful messages. I believe these films and messages can resonate on some level. It's all a matter of having it sink in. I think the only "message" that got a powerful hold on me were these anti-smoking advertisements that were shown on TV when I was in my early 30s. It featured a short Hispanic man talking through a hole in his throat using one of those electric razor things he stuck to his neck that gave him a robotic voice. He confessed painful things like, "I can't swim in a pool because I'll drown with this hole in my throat," except he sounded like an evil droid in *Star Wars*. After the 50th viewing of these commercials, I looked at the pack of cigarettes on my desk and said, "fuck it. I'm done."

Crazy

My wife called me crazy the other day. I used to take it as a compliment, to be being called crazy – but not anymore. The more I think about it, the more it hurts. It makes me depressed. She thinks I'm crazy and not necessarily in a good way. I'm driving her nuts with my craziness. That's what it comes down to. She wasn't like, "Oh, you're so crazy you lovable lug!" It was more like "You're crazy..." followed by a weary look of, "...and yes, it can be charming, but you're exhausting me." That's why it hurts. I'm driving her to exhaustion. The last thing I want is to make her feel bad. The thing is, she's right. I am crazy. I always thought it was just quirkiness, or nervous artistic energy, manic thoughts told aloud, or the occasional angry outburst. But I look back at my history and it's craziness.

Craziness is hard to define. Should I be locked up in a nut house? No. Do I need some sort of drug or tranquilizer? Yes.

Over the years I've self-medicated with mixed results. Cigarettes, booze, weed, cocaine, pain pills and other stimulants, tossed directly into the system, either separately or together, with varying results. But they didn't get to the heart of the craziness? What is craziness? What is *my* craziness? Can it be analyzed? Do I lack self-control? Are loud outbursts, wild mood swings, and lack of focus things that need to be identified and managed like anything else? Like the little check engine light on the car dashboard. It flashes and you pull the car over. Call the mechanic. Perhaps I should do the same. Self-realize I'm driving too fast, talking too loud, or mad about trivial things and need an official 'Time Out'.

Is it anger management? I'm not necessarily angry, but I do find myself mad at the world. If I had to fill out a dating app profile, I'd most-likely say I was happy, and fun-loving – but am I really? Maybe I'm lying to myself. I'd also say that I enjoy hiking and going to the movies, even though I only do those things once or twice a year. It's not my personality, but I do enjoy them. So, is it lying or is it stretching the truth? Pieces of the truth. The small samples aren't big enough to make the person, but if you string them all together, perhaps they complete the vision. They can become the building blocks of the person. The person I *really* am.

All these little things that merge to make a person, can also be all the little annoying habits I've encumbered that make me crazy.

Here lies the rub. If I try and curb my craziness, do I become someone else? I've tried to go stretches where I remain calm at everything that drives me nuts. I've managed my road rage and listen to every argument and retort with a clear-headed, rational thought. I've shrugged-off things like broken windows, flat tires, and lost money as "life." And you know what? I come across as someone in a light coma. As someone who has no fire in their gut. Downright boring.

Is my wife tired of that guy? The crazy guy? If I walk around like a meager, mild noodle whose heart rate is a persistent 80 beats per minute, will she be happy with him? How long will it take to get bored of that guy? What if she falls in love with him? Can I go back to who I was? Maybe she's in love with a different part of me. The person she fell in love with when I was acting normal so I could get a woman to settle down with me. You know? Like every person on a date before the Kraken comes out to play. Maybe she sees the good soul underneath the madness. The person I can become! The person she sees in me. The role model. The good dad. The excellent husband. The person she's trained over time with hard work and patience.

Where does edgy end and crazy begin? If you lose the edge, it's possible to be soft. Like the guy in the movies who seems meek and a bit of a push-over, then his family is attacked and he's a ruthless killer. Was he always a killer? Was the pent-up crazy ready to explode? If I tamp down the crazy, will it come out later in one explosive bang? If I let it seep out in spoon-sized doses, is it enough for others tolerate so they don't get caught in the one big bang of total craziness?

Admitting to being crazy is the first step to dealing with crazy. You don't want to, but that first step means pulling back and looking at yourself from afar. It's like when someone says you're being too loud. "I'm yelling?" you ask in a whisper. Then you keep your voice low. Same thing with crazy, although being called crazy feels like a personal attack. But still, that type of insult/realization takes time to digest. Once digested, you step back and say, "man, am I crazy?" Usually if everyone is crazy to you, it's probably because *you're* the crazy one. Similar to stomping around calling everyone a jerk. That's what jerks usually say.

How do you know you're crazy? Are crazy people lucid? Are they able to self-analyze their state of mind and their well-being?

I'm of the philosophy: "You gotta be crazy to make it in this crazy old world." Sounds like a line out of a 1950s movie, but that's my stance. Isn't it most people's stance? Who's walking around carefree and totally at ease? The second I step out the door, the world is a honking, screeching, twisted ball of fire coming right at me. How can one handle it with such calmness?

My son is super-duper mellow. I'm not sure where he got that mentality from. He's a New York basketball player with the mentality of a San Diego surfer. If he was any mellower, he'd be asleep. I admire his calmness, but it takes him 25 minutes to brush his teeth. Drives me crazy. Are we born crazy? I'm sure if he hangs around me long enough, he'll go crazy too. Environmental craziness by association. Inherited crazy. I'd say my father was crazy but he's just a pain in the ass. I developed my own crazy without his aid. My mother is crazier than him. Maybe I got some of her craziness. My sister is super mellow. I don't know how she escaped all the family craziness. Maybe she's crazy in a quiet way. That's what makes identifying crazy so difficult. Everyone looks normal, but they're all crazy inside.

What should I do about my craziness?

Well, I try to act less crazy, which makes me look crazier, but it's something I must do… for the sake of the family. Second, I must do everything I normally do and do the opposite. Instead of flying off the handle when something happens, I must contemplate what has happened and get over it rationally. My wife's favorite statement is "there's nothing you can do about it" and I hate that she's right. Of course she's right! Now I find myself walking around shrugging going "fuck it." Unfortunately, the longer you do that, the worse things get because you become apathetic to everything in the world. Forgot take out the garbage? Fuck it, I'll take it out in three days. Missed a car payment? Fuck it! Forgot to pay the taxes? Fuck it… Then, before you know it, you're living in the street.

Some people like to say: "God is testing my patience today," or, "Thank you, God for teaching me humility," which is a fine way to approach life, but I'm not sure I believe in God. (God, if you exist, don't read that last part). Crazy people don't like to be taught life lessons, they just chalk it up to bad luck, or the stupidity of mankind. Crazy people are "above it all" because they feel entitled to a smooth life path, and when it gets a little rocky, they lose their marbles.

Perhaps that's what crazy boils down to. The perception of reality. Obviously crazy people see the world in a different way, but who's to say it's not the right way? They're seeing their truth and that can't be wrong; can it?

Maybe there's a misdiagnosis going on with me. Being crazy and being DRIVEN crazy are two different things. If you've been driven, that insinuates that you can take the wheel and drive yourself back. *Real* crazy is downright crazy… pure crazy. But self-inflicted crazy is reversible. It's habitual crazy. Like smoking cigarettes or biting your toenails. You can stop to find some peace in the madness. That takes discipline.

I've always been of the mindset to fight crazy *with* crazy. I don't believe fighting crazy with reasonableness works. So, what's the solution? I think it's owning the crazy. Becoming one with the crazy so it's all part of one wholistic craziness that I can find peace in. The eye of the crazy storm.

It's just crazy enough to work.

Retirement Plan

At the rate I'm going, I estimate having around 11 cents in my savings account upon retiring. If you haven't been keeping up with the news, that won't buy much of anything. In fact, 11 cents might be more of a burden. Especially if it comes in heavy, cumbersome coins. Rattling copper is nothing but a nuisance. I challenge anyone to give 11 cents to a stranger on the street. It will be seen as nothing more than a collection of metal that will scratch the iPhone screen, short-circuit the key fob, and possibly combine with worthless paper receipts to form a small trash pile in the pocket of your jeans. As worthless as a bag of washers. So, my 11-cent retirement fund will be worth exactly nothing.

Nada.

Zilch.

The big, mother-fucking goose egg.

I don't know what investment firm you've hitched

your 401K to, but mine is most likely to be associated with Smith and Wesson. A glistening .44 magnum, which I'll use to blow the back of my head against the wall of a dive bar somewhere in a city where lonely hookers shrivel up and die, and the drunks of society go to murder their livers in a bye-bye of whiskey and rye. The kind of place where they push-broom the dead directly into the floor drain and don't think twice about it as they hose all the blood down to the very last drop. It's a fitting end to a life of misery and indentured servitude which we know as the everyday job. In other words, I'm most likely going to commit suicide so my family can reap the benefits of my insurance policy.

Don't worry! I'm not going to do this hideous act *today*. Probably more like 25 years from now. After the unmitigated, uncircumcised, unlubricated dick of life has reamed me in the ass for another quarter of a century. Then I'll put the retirement plan to my temple and pull the trigger. Hopefully it goes through the right parts. Knowing my luck, I'll blow a simple channel through my brain with no ill effects at all. Who needs another hole in the head? I just had one sewed up after brain surgery!

Maybe I'll turn myself into a drooling idiot, but that will make things worse. Then the people in my life will have to care for me, which defeats the point of *The Plan*. That kind of caretaking costs money. Perhaps I'll blowout half my memory… like the ability to remember who I am, and when people come to the door to collect my debts, I'll tell them I don't know who they're referring to. Maybe the damage will be nothing more than losing a small piece of my childhood memory, like my ability to remember the *Star Wars* films, then I can go back and watch them all over again for the first time. Wouldn't that be a delight?

I know what you're thinking… "A.J., you can't go around telling people your retirement plan is to blow your goddamn head off with a gun. The insurance company will render the policy null and void." But that's the beauty of my policy. It covers suicide! What luck! My uncle Ed actually designed *The Plan* for me and submitted all the paperwork to the insurance company. I don't understand any of that bullshit, but I assume he convinced them I was of sound mind and body and would never *dream* of doing such a dastardly deed.

A woman did come to my home to give me a blood test for drugs, which I passed somehow, and asked me a few questions. I don't remember any of the questions, but none were about suicide, and I don't think any of them even *mentioned* mental health. I have Trypanophobia, which is the fear of needles in a medical setting, so to draw blood, she had me lie on my couch to prevent vasovagal response, which is a fancy word for passing out. Once horizontal, I went into a state of tranquilized fear. She probably grilled me for info during that time and I blocked it out.

Her final assessment was that I was free-wheeling and completely sane. Perhaps her expertise was the ability to sniff out potential suicidal manic-depressives in one glance. Aren't most depressed people easy to spot? But if she did ask about the state of my mental health; what the hell was I going to say? That I'm one financial disaster away from visiting my local gun shop? Of course not! That's why we have a mental health crisis on our planet. No one talks about their mental health. It's embarrassing and screws up your life financially and renders all insurance policies worthless. It's best to keep your big, dumb, honest mouth shut.

Truth be told, I'm not particularly fond of the idea of eliminating myself in this fashion. But as it stands, I'll be working till I'm 85 as it is – my chin dragging on the ground as my back bends into a question mark. I'll be one of those poor old folks working at a fast-food joint because they have literally nothing, and living on the street won't work for them. You've seen these people. They're miserable. They see a pack of nutty teens blast through the door, and they become petrified from fear because it's possible the teens may crush them like a well-sucked cigarette. The old person looks at the teens and thinks: "I used to be you... seems like it was 15 minutes ago. I was cool, fucked like a rabbit, and had dreams of becoming a rock star. Now look at me! I'm on my deathbed assembling Happy Meals using Hollywood's latest plastic toy they spent 100 million dollars to promote, and I'm eating discount beans for every meal, and my medicine costs are higher than an NBA player's monthly salary." It's fucking terrifying.

There are many other ways I could execute *The Plan*, but I happen to handle a gun very well and I'm a good shot. Not that you need steady aim to hit your skull. You just stick the barrel directly to your head and squeeze. Maybe it's more of an anatomy thing. Knowing the best place to stick the barrel. I've heard the mouth is good and emptying the contents of your skull out back is most effective, but I've also heard going around the back, so the content come out the front is more effective. Who do I believe? I mean, anyone who's done this is most likely dead, so I can't interview them. They don't have a YouTube channel or a blog. I realize this is all very morbid, and the more I think about this, the more I realize there's more civil ways to complete *The Plan*. Besides, one can't buy a gun for 11 cents. I won't have enough money to purchase a solid steel, Grade-A American firearm on a fast-food paycheck… so *Plan B* of *The Plan* will take effect if necessary.

I could very easily step in front of a bus. At the frail age of 80, a bus could theoretically knock my head clean off like a bowling ball that hits the lane *next* to the lane I'm bowling in. But what if the driver is excellent, with keen eyes and ninja reflexes and hits the breaks and swerves before the full impact comes down on me? Again, I don't want to be a bag of broken bones needing 24/7 care. I want full elimination.

I could jump off the roof of a tall building, but then I may land on someone. I want this to be a clean exercise. I don't want to take out five people on my way to cashing in my policy. No one deserves to have an 80-year-old missile come blasting down on top of them. I could hang myself, but again, I've heard some tales of shock when that goes all wrong – a broken neck, but no death, or just a mangling of some sort that leaves the family with an image of horror. Pills seem like a peaceful way to go. I could gobble a bottle and go to bed. Everyone will say: "he passed peacefully in his sleep" and that would make me happy. Sure, people may be sad, but they won't be saying: "Why did he blast his face off with a gun onto the walls of that dive bar?" But what kind of pills should I take? I think headache medicine in large quantities just gives you a headache. I could gulp pain pills, but how do I get them? Off the street? From a doctor? Do I have to fake pain and have my general practitioner prescribe high-dosage Oxycodone pills? What is the answer here?

Perhaps I could approach the whole thing in a different way. I could live in the woods and let nature wear me to the bone, so I die from natural causes. Of course, I'm such a pussy, even at my current age a few hours without a warm shower and coffee causes me to fall apart. What will happen on the homestead trying to axe a tree down for firewood? I'll die from sadness before I've run out of food. Maybe that's the point. Still, it's not a great plan. I could drink myself to death, but I believe that could be a real labor-intensive journey. I drink a few glasses of wine and I fall asleep. I could pound a bottle of tequila, but I don't think that will kill me. I could run a hose into the window of my car and asphyxiate myself, but again, I don't want to leave a tortuous scene for my family to find. This needs to be clean and healthy. Almost like an accident.

Unfortunately, 11 cents will not purchase a hitman. I could leave a few bucks to the hitman after my wife cashes the check, but then she'd say: "Who's this guy getting 50 grand?" What if she refuses to pay? Will the hitman hit *her*? He could be a maniac! The guy *kills* people for a living, for God's sake! I can't bring some two-bit mercenary into the fold. I need simplicity and serenity. Like a man who gently lays where he is and places a white carnation on his chest and goes to sleep. I want that level of tranquility… a story-book ending. Knowing my luck, I'll hire a hitman off a fake hitman website and get arrested for hiring an undercover FBI agent posing as a hitman. Then I'll need to be bailed out, once again, defeating the purpose of *The Plan* as bail and lawyer fees cost money. You see those stories on the news all the time… woman hires a fake hitman from the web to knock off her husband – but it's an undercover cop. What do these people type into Google? Hitman for hire? Do they click on the first link in the results? Hitmen R Us? But, honestly, how much trouble could I reasonably get in? I'm hiring a guy to kill me! And it's not life insurance fraud… I'm allowed, to some degree, to kill myself, even if it's by the hand of someone else. Either way… cha-ching! (that's the sound of a cash register for those born after 2005).

But suicide isn't painless. Someone always suffers in the process… even if they're getting a large chunk of cash at the end. It will leave a hole in the heart for *someone*. Even if you disguise it as an accident, a murder, a passing in the sleep, or a tumble down a long, rocky cliff onto some jagged rocks. The United States really seems to enjoy keeping people alive, no matter how much they're suffering. Abortion and suicide are some of the worst infractions in the world, but if you need a warm meal or some medical attention, well, you can go fuck the hell off and die. Makes perfect sense, right? I don't want to make light of the subject, but what's a realist plan for retirement? Save money? I read an article that suggested saving about 2 million dollars to retire comfortably in my old age. 2 million dollars? As stated, I'm on the .11-dollar range. Then the article proceeded to list all the ways to invest my money, none of which I remember because it was completely irrelevant to my life. This was an article for people who make and SAVE money. Not folks living paycheck-to-paycheck.

Speaking of cliffs and jagged rocks, I always thought a fiery car crash would be a great way to go. I could drive to California where there seems to be a ton of long and winding roads on steep and rocky cliffs to speed right off the side, plummeting to my death. In the 1960s, The Beach Boys and 30 other bands sang songs about these roads. Dead Man's Curve and all the Jazz. Again, knowing my luck (did I mention I have bad luck?) I'll fly right over the railing and nose-dive into a boulder, and nothing will happen. Airbags will deploy, and I'll suffer a basic mangling. An ambulance ride costs 10 grand for some reason, and a stay in the hospital can cost 2 million bucks for a few days in traction. Isn't America great? I'm sure in Italy or Switzerland you can retire with a loaf of bread and half a glass of wine and feel completely comfortable knowing the government and your neighbors will take care of you. In America, you can't go more than 15 minutes without needing to pay for some life-saving, or at least *life-moving* item. Pretty soon we'll be paying for air. Cars, unfortunately for *The Plan* purposes, are built very well. On TV shows in the 1970s, a car would explode the second its wheels left the highway, tumbling down the California cliffs like children barrel-rolling down a grass hill, engulfed in flames and all six of its gas tanks igniting in a nuclear blast that could be seen from space. But reality and fiction are not the same. It's *really* hard to light a car on fire. My Jeep was designed to avoid death because a gaggle of engineers spent decades crashing Jeeps into walls and studying the results. So, unless I buy a 1975 Ford Pinto, now considered vintage and worth more money than I have, crashing my car into a funeral pyre seems fruitless.

The goal here is to execute *The Plan* (and myself) to full effect while avoiding as much suffering as humanly possible… for myself *and* others. I believe I will avoid all senseless violence like bar fights where I could be knifed in the neck, Gym altercations where I could be knocked in the skull with a 45 pound dumbbell, and any road rage incidents where some malcontent with a huge bald eagle American flag emblazoned on the back window of his truck mistakes patriotism with privilege and axes me in the chest because I merged into traffic ahead of him, emasculating him, and embarrassing all his children and grandchildren coming down the pipe. These scenarios may be convenient for my purposes, but I prefer to go out on my own accord.

As you may know, there's a huge faction of people who believe I'll have to answer to a higher calling about *The Plan*. No, not the IRS… God himself. Or herself. Whichever you prefer. Sure, I may leave a bounty for my family on earth; but what will the verdict be at the pearly gates? What's the price? One way ticket to hell? I have never read the Bible, the Quran, or the Torah, but I believe they all frown upon suicide. I'm not sure. I'm agnostic, so I don't know what to believe, but it might be wise to err on the side of caution.

Even though *The Plan* is the end plan for immediate results, I could play the long game. Absolve myself of smite, karma, or some other kismet kiss of death… so to speak. I want to die around 80, but perhaps I can start now. Maybe if I eat a pound of bacon every day, by the time I'm 80, my heart will be 90 percent bacon fat and will fail right on cue. But I don't want a life of bad health. I want to enjoy the ride before the end comes. I'm not suicidal in the traditional sense, I just want the end result to come at the right time. Sure, I'm depressed about my finances, but I'm not *depressed* depressed. If anything, I'm fairly happy… especially about my Retirement Plan. I believe it's rock solid. Not rocky *cliff* rock solid, but a decent enough plan that it will work out. Iron clad, even.

I have 25-30 years to figure it out. Maybe the moment will present itself as it's happening… skiing off a cliff, or a swan dive into the Grand Canyon.

The possibilities are endless.